W9-CEK-004

INTO THE
MUMMY'S TOMB

Text © 1992 Nicholas Reeves and The Madison Press Limited
Jacket, Design and Compilation © 1992 The Madison Press Limited

All rights reserved. No part of this book may be reproduced or transmitted in any form or by any means, electronic or mechanical, including photocopying and recording, or by any information retrieval system, without written permission from the copyright holders, except for brief passages quoted by a reviewer in a newspaper or magazine.

First published in the United States by
Scholastic Inc., 730 Broadway
New York, N.Y. 10003

SCHOLASTIC HARDCOVER is a registered trademark of Scholastic Inc.

Library of Congress Cataloging-in-Publication Data
Reeves, Nicholas.
    Into the Mummy's tomb: the real-life discovery of Tutankhamun's treasures / by Nicholas Reeves with Nan Froman.
        p.   cm.
    Summary: An account of Howard Carter's discovery of the tomb of King Tutankhamun, descriptions of the artifacts inside and their importance, the discovery in 1988 of more artifacts, and theories about the curse associated with the tomb.
    ISBN 0-590-45752-7
    1. Tutankhamen, King of Egypt — Tomb — Juvenile literature.
2. Egypt — Antiquities — Juvenile literature. (1. Tutankhamen, King of Egypt — Tomb. 2.Egypt — Antiquities.) I. Froman, Nan. II. Title.
DT87.5.R44 1992
932'.014 — dc20   91-46186 CIP AC

Design and Art Direction: Gordon Sibley Design Inc.
Illustration: Stephen Hutchings, Jack McMaster, Margo Stahl
Editorial Director: Hugh M. Brewster
Project Editor: Mireille Majoor
Production Director: Susan Barrable
Production Assistant: Donna Chong
Printer: Arti Grafiche Motta S.p.A

Endpapers: Women weep in front of mummies in their coffins at the Opening of the Mouth ceremony. This ceremony was supposed to give back to the mummies all the senses and abilities they had when alive.
Previous page: This wooden model of the head of the boy pharaoh shows him being born from the lotus flower like the Egyptian sun god.
Right: The gold funeral mask of Tutankhamun was placed over the mummified head of the king.
Overleaf: King Tutankhamun is depicted as a fierce warrior in this scene from a brightly painted chest found in his tomb.

Produced by Madison Press Books
40 Madison Avenue
Toronto, Ontario
Canada M5R 2S1

Printed in Italy   *First Scholastic printing, October 1992*

INTO THE
MUMMY'S TOMB

BY NICHOLAS REEVES
WITH NAN FROMAN

A SCHOLASTIC/MADISON PRESS BOOK

CONTENTS

For Kate, Elizabeth, Harriet and their friends

Below the cliffs of the Valley of the Kings the royal funeral procession moves slowly in the burning sun. Workers strain at the ropes as they haul the heavy gold coffin containing the mummified body of their king, Tutankhamun. A gilded throne, decorated chests and carved furniture are carried by weeping mourners toward steps cut into the desert floor. These steps lead downward to an underground tomb. There, surrounded by his kingly possessions, the spirit of the pharaoh will live on for eternity.

At last the moment Howard Carter has dreamed of has arrived. The heavy lid of King Tutankhamun's coffin has been lifted. Inside it is a second golden coffin. Carter gently reaches down and brushes away the remains of a decayed linen shroud. Within this coffin lies a third coffin containing the mummified body of the pharaoh. Soon Howard Carter will stare into the face of the young king of ancient Egypt who was buried on that warm spring day more than three thousand years before.

FORGOTTEN TREASURES

LONDON, ENGLAND, 1988

These ancient Egyptian carved heads were among the treasures discovered by Howard Carter and Lord Carnarvon that had been missing for many years.

"Can I help you, sir?" The voice made me jump. "Yes, yes, I hope you can!" I had been called in to Sotheby's, the art auction house, to identify some historic objects. Suddenly I noticed a table in the corner covered with unusual artifacts I knew at once were from ancient Egypt. I picked up a painted wooden head and my heart began to beat faster. From its cobra headdress and long black beard I knew it was the image of an Egyptian pharaoh, Amenophis III, the grandfather of King Tutankhamun.

"Where did these things come from?" I asked the Sotheby's sales clerk. "Archaeologists have been looking for them ever since they were found in Egypt decades ago. Oh, my name is Nicholas Reeves. I'm from the British Museum," I added, since he seemed a little startled by my excitement.

"I believe they were sent to us from Highclere Castle by Lord Carnarvon."

"Carnarvon," I replied. "Of course!"

I knew that the Lord Carnarvon living at Highclere Castle today was the grandson of the Lord Carnarvon who in 1922, along with Egyptologist Howard Carter, had made the most spectacular find in the history of archaeology—the tomb of King Tutankhamun.

I'd first heard about Carnarvon and Carter and their amazing discovery when I was fourteen. I was working part-time cataloging the Egyptian artifacts at my local museum, and on rainy afternoons the museum archaeologists would tell stories of adventure in Egypt. Howard Carter was one of their heroes. In 1917 Carter was convinced that there was still one royal tomb in Egypt that no one had yet uncovered. He persuaded Lord Carnarvon to back him in the search for the lost tomb of the boy pharaoh, Tutankhamun. After years of searching, the two men discovered Tutankhamun's burial place, overflowing with dazzling treasures, where it had lain undisturbed for over three thousand years.

The story of Carnarvon and Carter was the beginning of my fascination with ancient Egypt. I studied archaeology at university and eventually became an Egyptologist—an archaeologist with a special interest in the land of the pharaohs. I soon began working at the British Museum,

(*Right*) I stand outside Highclere Castle (*above*), where the Carnarvon family has lived for generations. No one could have guessed how many Egyptian artifacts were still to be found inside the castle.

where I was one of the people in charge of a fabulous collection of Egyptian treasures. I knew the objects I'd seen at Sotheby's had been unearthed by Lord Carnarvon and Howard Carter in the years before they had discovered Tutankhamun's tomb. And archaeologists ever since had wondered what had happened to them.

A few days later I was at my museum desk when the telephone rang. It was Lord Carnarvon's secretary calling from Highclere Castle.

"Lord Carnarvon is anxious to get an expert's opinion on the objects from his grandfather's collection," she explained. "Sotheby's told us of your interest and we'd like you to come to Highclere and look them over. If it would be convenient, that is."

Convenient! I almost laughed out loud. I was itching to learn just what missing treasures might be found at Highclere. Lord Carnarvon's secretary told me that his lordship wanted to put the treasures on display at the castle. My job would be to sort and identify various objects, write a detailed description of each one and arrange them for the display.

"Of course it would be convenient," I said with a smile. "How soon would you like me to be there?"

When I arrived at Highclere the butler ushered me into the castle's grand entrance hall. Looking up at the high vaulted ceiling, I felt as if I were in a cathedral. Lord Carnarvon greeted me and we walked briskly through room after room full of elaborate furniture, past walls covered with paintings of his ancestors.

"Can you tell me how you found the objects?" I asked him.

"Certainly," he replied. "Last year I decided to make a list of the valuable items in the castle—the furniture, paintings, fine china and silver. To help me, I called in a team of experts from Sotheby's and my father's retired butler.

"We spent days going through the castle room by room. At last I thought we had finished. As I walked through the rooms one last time with the butler, I remember saying, 'Well that's it then.'

" 'Yes my lord,' the butler replied, 'except for the Egyptian stuff.'

" 'I looked at him in amazement. 'What Egyptian stuff? There is no Egyptian stuff!'

"But with a gleam in his eye he replied, 'Oh yes there is!' He then led me to this unused doorway connecting the smoking room and the drawing room. We moved a table which had been placed in front of the door and unlocked it. Beyond was a secret passageway with another door at the end!"

Lord Carnarvon opened the door and I could see what he meant.

"I had no idea it was here," he continued. "I was sure I knew every nook and cranny of the castle. As you can see, on either side of the passage are these hidden cupboards. The butler opened one of them and pulled out an Egyptian cigarette tin. He lifted the lid and, to my astonishment, revealed the glistening blue beads of an ancient necklace. I pulled out another tin and peered inside. The bronze figure of an Egyptian god stared back at me."

As Lord Carnarvon spoke I could see that there were

(Above) The present Lord Carnarvon (right) and his father's retired butler, Robert Taylor (left), stand by the secret cupboards where ancient Egyptian treasures, like the ones below, had been hidden for decades.

small compartments in each cupboard, going back as far as an arm could reach. He explained that each one had contained tin boxes and cotton wool full of the ancient treasures I had seen at Sotheby's!

"My father must not have known the objects were here. He'd never let us even mention Egypt," said Lord Carnarvon. "The butler thinks it was because of all that superstitious talk about my grandfather's death and the mummy's curse."

Afterwards we toured the castle—both downstairs in the servants' domain where I would eventually set up the display, and upstairs in the old family quarters. Inside one room, behind the dusty glass of a large bookcase, I noticed a strange-looking pile of bits of wood lying in brown straw.

"I really must have all this cleared away," said Lord Carnarvon.

I looked more closely at the fragments of wood. "Just a moment, Lord Carnarvon," I said. "This wood looks very old to me." I began to pick up the fragments and could soon see that they fit together. "These are the pieces of two ancient jewel boxes!" I exclaimed. I recognized them from photographs I had seen in an old book about Howard Carter's excavations in Egypt. "I thought they had been lost forever." The idea that they had nearly been thrown away made me shudder.

From that day on the castle was turned inside out. Who knew what other treasures might be lying about, gathering dust? Lord Carnarvon found a miniature bronze axehead stuck to the paint on a windowsill. In another room was a beautiful jar made of milky-white alabaster that had once held oil used in Egyptian burial preparations. In the housekeeper's room we found a stone fragment covered with hieroglyphs, the ancient Egyptians' picture writing. And inside a gun cabinet was a tiny stone head. Highclere Castle was full of surprises.

Before I began my work that first day, Lord Carnarvon

and I sat down for lunch in the richly decorated library. "This is the room where my grandfather and Howard Carter would meet to discuss their excavations in the Valley of the Kings," Lord Carnarvon told me.

I suddenly felt very much like Howard Carter, who had worked for the present lord's grandfather, discovering, sorting and conserving the thousands of beautiful objects found in Tutankhamun's tomb.

"And what a discovery they made!" I replied, biting into a sandwich.

The unbelievably rich tomb of the boy king Tutankhamun is the greatest archaeological find of all time. No one before or since has ever discovered a royal mummy laid to rest in such splendor. Inside the tomb Carter and Carnarvon found priceless treasures—golden statues, jewels, gilded furniture, beautifully carved alabaster lamps and vases, ivory and ebony caskets and more—all made by Egypt's most gifted craftsmen. These treasures have fascinated the world since the day they were found.

But Lord Carnarvon and Howard Carter were to spend many frustrating years searching before they struck the first of the creamy-white stone steps leading to the royal tomb.

The library at Highclere Castle *(top)* where Lord Carnarvon *(left inset)* and Howard Carter *(right inset)* planned their digs in Egypt. *(Bottom)* They found these model tools and dishes outside the tomb of King Amenophis III in 1915.

CHAPTER ONE

THE HIDDEN STEPS
CAIRO, EGYPT, 1907

Lord Carnarvon fumbled with his pocket watch as his car slowly made its way through the crowded streets of Cairo. It was market day and his driver had to weave around braying donkeys and wooden carts laden with vegetables and fruit. At almost every turn a turbanned merchant rapped at the window, offering him cloth, spices or a cup of sweet tea.

"I'm going to be late again," he muttered to himself. He was on his way to see the Director of the Egyptian Antiquities Service. This official gave out licenses permitting people to dig for ancient artifacts.

Lord Carnarvon spent every winter in Egypt, far from his home at Highclere Castle. As a young man he had loved driving fast cars, but a serious crash had left him in poor health. His doctors had told him that the damp English weather was the worst thing for him and had recommended a hot, dry climate. Carnarvon chose Egypt.

Egypt was full of wealthy North Americans and Europeans who spent their time digging up the desert in search of ancient artifacts. Occasionally they found priceless treasures, and Lord Carnarvon, who had always been interested in archaeology, was

Cairo's marketplace is still as crowded and lively today as it was when Lord Carnarvon lived in Egypt.

soon gripped by the excitement of the hunt. He too took up excavation to pass his time in a pleasant and profitable way.

And so Carnarvon had hired a foreman and a team of workmen for his first dig. After six weeks of back-breaking labor all they found was an ancient mummified cat in its cat-shaped wooden coffin. But Lord Carnarvon was not discouraged. He decided that he simply needed a better place to excavate. He would see what the director might be able to offer him for the next season.

"Good morning, Lord Carnarvon. How good to see you again," the director said. "I understand you are looking for a new place to dig."

"Yes, I am," replied Carnarvon. "I didn't have too much luck last year," he said with a wry smile, "but I'm confident that given a new spot this season will be much more successful. I've also heard that you know of someone who might be interested in digging with me."

"We can, of course, find a new excavation site for you, my lord, and yes, I would like to suggest that you employ the services of a friend of mine. His name is Howard Carter, a very knowledgeable man. I'm sure you'll find him helpful."

Howard Carter had first come to Egypt at the age of seventeen with a British Egyptologist who had noticed his talents as a draftsman. Soon Carter's skills were in demand at several excavation sites, where he would make precise drawings of the tombs and ancient objects that were uncovered. After a few years' hard work he found himself in charge of teams of workmen clearing tombs. He learned to speak Arabic, so that he could talk to the Egyptian workers, and he taught himself how to read hieroglyphs. If anyone could help Lord Carnarvon find treasures in the vast, barren desert, it was Howard Carter.

"But let me warn you, my lord," the director added, "my friend is an extremely stubborn man."

"I'd like to meet your Mr. Carter," replied Carnarvon. "A stubborn man is a determined one, after all."

Lord Carnarvon and Howard Carter made a perfect excavating team. While Carnarvon had the money to fund the digs, Carter had the necessary practical skills and knowledge of Egyptology. From the outset they both knew they wanted to dig in the Valley of the Kings—the burial ground of the ancient Egyptian pharaohs. Here they were convinced they could find the most fabulous treasures imaginable. But

Howard Carter (center) inherited his talent as an artist from his father, who was also a painter. His abilities came to the attention of a British Egyptologist who brought young Carter to Egypt in 1891. Over the years, Carter gained enormous experience in making accurate pictures of ancient Egyptian objects and tomb paintings (above right, left). Before long he was supervising digging and exploration.

Egypt is a desert country in the north of Africa. During ancient times, most of its major cities, tombs

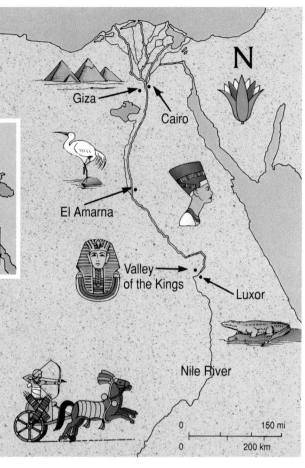

and palaces were built along the banks of the river Nile. The ruins of many of these still exist and can be visited by tourists today.

The earliest Egyptians dug shallow pits in the desert where they buried their dead with just a few jars of food for nourishment in the next world. The hot, dry sand of the desert dehydrated and preserved bodies so well that some of them are still in good condition today. This sand-dried body is more than five thousand years old.

the right to dig in this area had already been granted to an American millionaire, Theodore Davis. There was nothing that Carnarvon and Carter could do but dig elsewhere.

Over the next few years they uncovered two lost temples and excavated several important tombs. They found many artifacts, some of which were later hidden at Highclere Castle. The digs were successful because Howard Carter was willing to roll up his sleeves along with the workmen. He was always there to read the smallest clue in the objects sifted from the dust. The work was exhausting and could be dangerous too. At one site poisonous cobras hissed at the workers with every shovelful of earth that was moved.

In 1915 they were allowed to dig at the tomb of King Amenophis III. This tomb, like all the other royal tombs ever discovered, had been plundered by robbers. But Howard Carter was convinced that there was one royal tomb lying untouched in the valley—the tomb of the boy king, Tutankhamun.

Tutankhamun had become king of all Egypt more than three thousand years before when he was only nine years old. His reign was neither easy nor long. Pharaoh Akhenaten, who had reigned before Tutankhamun and was probably his father, had insisted that the people of Egypt worship only one god instead of paying tribute to the many gods they had always believed in. This change in the old system of religion had been very unpopular. And so, once Akhenaten died, Tutankhamun had the difficult task of restoring the old religion. Because he was so young he shared his power with two older men in the court, Ay and Horemheb. But the boy king died at the age of eighteen, and Ay took the throne.

THE PYRAMIDS

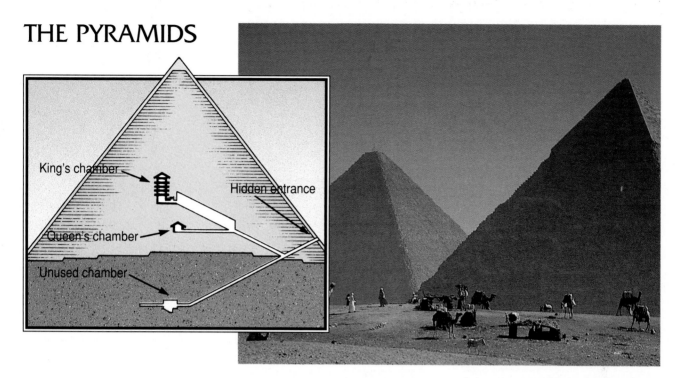

King's chamber

Hidden entrance

Queen's chamber

Unused chamber

It was very important to the ancient Egyptians that a dead king's body not be disturbed after it had been laid to rest. By the time Tutankhamun died, pharaohs no longer built pyramid tombs because the huge structures quickly attracted thieves who broke in looking for gold and tore the sacred mummies apart in search of jewels. Not even the long tunnels and hidden doorway of the great pyramid of King Cheops at Giza *(above left)* could the keep a pharaoh's treasures safe. The ancient robbers did their work well: today every pyramid in Egypt is empty *(above right)*.

The reason for Tutankhamun's early death remains a mystery. Many have wondered if Ay, in his eagerness to become king, murdered the child-pharaoh.

Carter knew that Tutankhamun would have been buried in a hidden tomb cut deep into the rock of the Valley of the Kings as was the custom at that time in Egypt. He kept track of all the discoveries made there over the years. The one pharaoh's tomb that no one had ever found was that of Tutankhamun.

Tutankhamun would have been laid to rest with everything he needed to survive in the afterlife. By studying ancient papyri and the fragments of objects already found in other tombs, Carter knew that these treasures would surpass anything anyone had seen before—there would be gilded furniture for the king to rest upon, chariots for hunting and warfare, bows and arrows, rich clothing, games, food and wine. He expected that the mummy, covered with jewels, would lie inside a carved stone sarcophagus surrounded by ornately decorated shrines.

If he and Lord Carnarvon could find Tutankhamun's tomb, they would be the first ever to find out how the ancient

Egyptians buried their kings. And if they found papyrus rolls in Tutankhamun's tomb, perhaps they could shed some light on his troubled reign. History could be rewritten!

Because of the First World War, it wasn't until 1917 that the way was finally clear for Carter and Carnarvon to begin a thorough search of the Valley of the Kings.

Early one morning Carter rode by donkey into the lonely, silent valley. Soon a procession of men and boys appeared on the road, their long white robes fluttering in the breeze. The sound of Arabic wafted through the air.

"Mr. Carter, hello!"

Carter looked up and waved to Ahmed Gurgar, the head *reis* or foreman of the work party. "Come on over, Reis Ahmed, so we can go through our plan of attack."

The two men squatted down and spread a large map of the Valley of the Kings out in front of them. A difficult task lay ahead. Much of the ground had been overturned by other excavators, but there were no records of which areas had already been explored. Carter decided they would have to clear the whole valley down to bedrock.

As the days progressed and the sun beat down mercilessly, hundreds of men moved thousands of tons of limestone rubble with picks, hoes and their bare hands. There was so much rock to move that Carter ordered tracks laid down for a hand-propelled railway. Soon the workmen were pushing carts of broken rock across the valley.

By the end of that first season the team had found nothing. The second and third seasons passed but still Carter found no sign of Tutankhamun's tomb. In 1920, the only discovery was a cache of thirteen beautiful alabaster jars. Like all the previous years, 1921 brought no important discoveries.

The workmen became more bored and discouraged each year. Carter was certain the tomb was in the Valley of the Kings, but he could see that Lord Carnarvon was losing patience.

HIGHCLERE CASTLE, HAMPSHIRE, ENGLAND, 1922

"**M**r. Carter! Good to see you again, sir. Please come into the library and I'll tell his lordship that you've arrived," said the butler.

"Carter, welcome back to England! How are you?" Lord Carnarvon smiled heartily as he came into the library, his little terrier Susie padding close on his heels. The two men exchanged news about their health, the weather and Carter's sea voyage from Egypt until Carter thought he couldn't bear it another minute.

But then Carnarvon's voice dropped a little and he bent forward thoughtfully to scratch the terrier's ears. "I must admit, I asked you here because I think we need to have a chat about our work in the valley."

"I suspected as much, my lord, and..."

"The truth of the matter is," Carnarvon said hurriedly, "I simply cannot put up the funds for another season of digging. As you know, the expense is considerable. We've been at it for five years now and have come up with nothing. I think you'll have to agree that the Valley of the Kings does not hold the tomb of Tutankhamun."

Carter took a deep breath and pulled a folded, frayed map from his jacket pocket. It was the map of the valley that they had used over the years. He spread it carefully over his knees, smoothing it down with his hands. Clearing his throat, he said, "There's just this one last triangle of ground that we haven't explored yet, my lord. It's here, near the tomb of Ramesses VI." He brought the map to Carnarvon and traced the area with his fingertip. "As long as there's an untouched spot in the valley, we've got to continue our search."

"I'm sorry to disappoint you, Carter, but I really have made up my mind."

Carter looked up at Lord Carnarvon, his dark eyes burning. "If you are agreeable, my lord, I'd like to put up the money for one more season myself. And if I do find the tomb, the discovery will still belong to you since the license is in your name."

Carnarvon stared at the map for a few moments, and then looked at Howard Carter shrewdly as he lit a cigarette. Finally he said, "That's a very generous offer, Carter, but we can't have

When the pharaohs realized that neither their treasures nor their mummies would be safe from thieves in pyramids, they looked for a better place to build their tombs. The Valley of the Kings, with its natural pyramid-shaped peak *(above)*, seemed an ideal location. Secret chambers were cut deep into the rock and their entrances were covered with rubble and sand. But thieves were able to find even these hidden tombs. By the time Lord Carnarvon started digging it was believed that all the burial places had been robbed. In his first season digging among the tombs, all that he found was a mummified cat in a wooden coffin *(far left)*. By 1920 his only discovery in the Valley of the Kings was a group of alabaster oil jars *(left)*.

that, can we? I give in—we'll keep digging, but for one more season only. I will, of course, continue to foot the bill."

Carter breathed a sigh of relief. Funding another excavation season would have taken all the money he had and more. Now he had one last chance to find the royal tomb.

Howard Carter returned to Egypt as soon as he could. His servant, Abdul Ali, and the head foreman, Reis Ahmed, met him at the train station in Luxor.

Carter smiled wearily when he saw them. "We've got one more chance," he said.

A sweet trilling sound suddenly came from one of Carter's bundles. Abdul and Reis Ahmed looked quizzically at Carter, who lifted a blanket revealing a brilliant yellow canary in its cage.

"A golden bird!" Reis Ahmed exclaimed. "God willing, it will lead us to the tomb, sir."

Over the next few days Carter and Reis Ahmed carefully planned their strategy for the season's work. They would start digging near the tomb of Ramesses VI, where they had struck the ancient remains of the huts of workers who had built that pharaoh's tomb. In a few days they had removed the hut foundations and were ready to dig out the remaining three feet of rubble down to the bedrock.

The next morning when Carter arrived at the site, he was greeted by a strange silence. No one was talking or singing; in fact no one was even working. There must have been an accident, he thought with a sick feeling. He quickly dismounted from his donkey.

"Mr. Carter..." Reis Ahmed began walking toward him. The foreman was being followed by the shy water boy.

"Yes, what is it? What has happened?" Carter snapped, expecting the worst. He cast an eye over the small boy but could see nothing wrong with him.

"Please, Mr. Carter, the water boy has found a step cut into the rock." Reis Ahmed then quickly explained how the boy had been kicking at the earth with his heel, making a place to set jars of cool water in the ground, when he had struck something

Howard Carter's pet canary was killed by a cobra soon after he discovered the tomb in the Valley of the Kings.

hard and sharp. He had called the foreman over, and in no time the workers had uncovered a step.

His heart pounding, Carter ran over to the spot where a large group of workmen had gathered. There it was—a creamy-white step. Could it possibly be the entrance to Tutankhamun's tomb? He was filled with a surge of energy and impatience. "Back to work, back to work," he shouted in Arabic at the top of his voice. "But please dig carefully now." Throwing off his jacket and grabbing a pick, Carter began to help his men.

By the end of the next day they had cleared twelve steps.

The steps led straight down in the style of tomb entrances built during the time of Tutankhamun. At the bottom was a door made of stone blocks which had been covered with plaster. Carter could see that the plaster had been stamped by the ancient cemetery priests with large royal seals showing a jackal over nine captives. He knew this meant that the tomb had been built for somebody important, but who? He ran his hands over the seals searching for clues.

More than anything else, Carter wanted to break the doorway down, but darkness was falling. He chose his most trustworthy men to stand guard at the tomb entrance and rode home by moonlight.

Questions raced through his mind. Did the steps lead to the tomb of an Egyptian noble? Or perhaps to a hiding place where a royal mummy had been moved out of the reach of tomb robbers? He could not dare hope that he had at last found the tomb of Tutankhamun. But he did know one thing for certain—the unbroken plaster on the door proved that whatever was inside the tomb had lain undisturbed since ancient times.

The next morning Carter went into Luxor and sent off a telegram to Lord Carnarvon. He also sent one to Arthur Callender, an old friend who was an architect and engineer. Carter knew he could rely on Callender to help him in the months ahead if he had made an important discovery.

Back at the site Carter had his workers fill in the excavation and roll boulders on top of it. As much as he wanted to break down the door immediately, Carter felt he should wait until Lord Carnarvon, who had paid for the search, was in Egypt to witness the opening. Soon there was no sign of the tomb.

At Highclere Castle, Lord Carnarvon and his daughter, Lady Evelyn, were drinking tea in the library when the butler entered with an envelope on a silver tray. Carnarvon picked it up hastily when he noticed it was a telegram and ripped it open. Lady Evelyn read over his shoulder:

AT LAST HAVE MADE WONDERFUL DISCOVERY IN VALLEY; A MAGNIFICENT TOMB WITH SEALS INTACT; RE-COVERED SAME FOR YOUR ARRIVAL; CONGRATULATIONS. CARTER.

"How about a trip to Egypt, Eve?" Carnarvon said with a smile.

When Carter arrived home that evening he was exhausted. He hadn't eaten or slept for what seemed like days, and he was looking forward to a cool bath. But he was met at his door by Abdul Ali who held a few yellow feathers in his fingers. The servant's eyes were large with fear.

"The golden bird has been killed by a cobra," he blurted out.

"What a shame. Well, make sure the snake is out of the house."

Abdul caught Carter by the sleeve, "The pharaoh's serpent ate the bird because it led us to the hidden tomb."

"What? That's superstitious nonsense!" scoffed Carter.

"You must not disturb the tomb," Abdul insisted, and brushing past Carter, he slipped away into the night.

After a few hours of digging, it was clear that the steps led to the entrance of a tomb cut into the rock *(below)*. Howard Carter made this drawing of a seal showing a jackal over nine bound captives *(left)* which was stamped into the plaster of the doorway. He knew that this seal was only placed on the doorways of royal tombs. But whose tomb was this?

CHAPTER TWO

THE DAY OF DAYS
THE VALLEY OF THE KINGS, EGYPT, 1922

"Hello, here we are," Lady Evelyn cried, waving from the window of the train as it pulled into Luxor station.

Two and a half weeks after Carter sent off his telegram, Carnarvon and his daughter had finally arrived in Egypt. Carter walked along the platform to greet them. At last, he thought, I'll be able to see what is on the other side of that plastered doorway.

Lord Carnarvon stepped from the train stiffly and leaned forward on his cane. "Well Carter, what have you found for us?" he asked.

"I'd like to show you at once, my lord, unless you're too tired."

"Nonsense. We're keen to visit the site, aren't we, Eve?" Carnarvon smiled at his daughter.

After what seemed an endless wait for the ferry, Carter, Carnarvon, and Lady Evelyn crossed the Nile and then climbed on the donkeys which would take them to the Valley of the Kings. Arthur Callender had supervised the clearing of the steps and tomb

(Inset, left to right) Lady Evelyn, Lord Carnarvon, Howard Carter and Arthur Callender stand at the top of the staircase *(top)* leading to the mysterious plastered doorway.

entrance in time for their arrival.

"How exciting!" Lady Evelyn exclaimed a little nervously when she saw the cleanly-cut steps descending into the dark ground. In the falling light they examined the mysterious seals on the plastered door. It was too late in the day to continue the hard work of digging out the last few steps, so the little party agreed to meet at the site the next morning.

Carter and his friends were at the tomb entrance shortly after sunrise. The Egyptian workers were delighted to see Lord Carnarvon back in the valley and they smiled and waved when they saw him. Even Carter was impressed by how fast his team worked as they dug out the remaining steps and removed debris from around the plastered door. Everyone was anxious to see what lay behind it. Lord Carnarvon paced about smoking, while Carter directed the diggers.

At last Carter could see the whole doorway. He bent down once again to examine the ancient seals that had been uncovered in the morning's digging. Lord Carnarvon

(Above) Rubble from the filled-in corridor was carted away in basketfuls by a line of young boys. Buried in this rubble, Carter found a beautiful painted wooden model of the young pharaoh's head rising from a lotus flower like the Egyptian sun god (right).

and Lady Evelyn stood just behind him. The seals at the bottom of the door were much less blurry, and Carter could read the name on several of them.

"Tutankhamun!" he read aloud in awe. Had he at last found the hidden tomb of the boy pharaoh?

"But look," Carter continued, his heart sinking, "part of the door has been opened and reclosed." He pointed to the top left-hand corner where there was a patch in the plaster. "Someone must have entered the tomb after it had been sealed."

"Ancient tomb robbers, no doubt," suggested Carnarvon grimly. "It looks as though it has been opened twice. Here's another patch in the plaster."

Carter didn't know what to think. He feared that the tomb had indeed been robbed, stripped of all its valuables.

Trying to conceal his fear, he sat down with his sketchpad and made careful drawings of the door and the seals on it while Lord Carnarvon took photographs. Then, block by block, they broke down the stone doorway. Behind the ancient wall stretched a sloping passage filled from floor to ceiling with limestone rubble. They could see that a tunnel had once been dug through this rubble, and that it too had been refilled long ago. Carter was certain that this tunnel

had been made by robbers on their way into the tomb.

It took the workers nearly two days to empty the passage. The strongest men shovelled the limestone chips into baskets. A long line of boys passed the heavy baskets along the corridor and up the steps where they were emptied outside the tomb entrance. Mixed in with the pieces of limestone were several fascinating objects. Carter picked up one of these—the head of the young king rising out of a lotus flower made of painted wood. Perhaps it had been dropped by the thieves as they fled.

At the far end of the passage was a second plaster-covered doorway stamped with the priests' seals. Some of the seals bore the name of Tutankhamun. This door's top left-hand corner also showed signs of having been opened and then repaired. The opening would have been the perfect size for someone to squeeze through.

Carter chipped away at the plaster and stone with an iron rod until there was a small hole in the door. He inserted the rod. There seemed to be empty space beyond.

"Light the candle," he said. Lady Evelyn handed him a candle and, with trembling hands, he put it through the hole to test for foul gases. It was safe—the flame remained lit. Carter widened the hole a little and putting the candle back inside, he peered through. The candle flame flickered briefly as hot air escaped from the chamber. As it steadied, light penetrated the inky darkness of the room for the first time in over three thousand years. A few seconds passed, and then a few more.

"Can you see anything?" Lord Carnarvon asked anxiously.

"Yes," breathed Carter, unable to tear himself away from the peephole, "wonderful things!" Once his eyes had adjusted to the dim light, Carter was able to make sense of the mysterious shadows and shapes within the room. There were gilded wooden animals, statues and gold—everywhere he looked there was the gleam of gold!

Pulling himself away, Carter widened the hole so that they could all look through.

"Shall we go in?" he asked, already breaking apart more of the plaster.

A few minutes later Carnarvon, Carter, Lady Evelyn and Arthur Callender climbed through the hole and stepped carefully down into the room. They felt like intruders in someone else's home. A faint smell of sweet perfume and oil lingered inside the stuffy chamber. It looked as though someone had been there just a few days ago—here was a blackened lamp, and there on the floor was a garland of dried flowers. They looked so fresh that Carter had to remind himself they had been left there over three thousand years before.

At first no one could speak. The light from their candles moved crazily about as they tried to take in the wonders

His first brief glimpse into the dimly lit tomb was enough to show Howard Carter that he had found something no one else has seen for over three thousand years: the dazzling treasure-filled tomb of an Egyptian pharaoh, just as the ancient priests had left it.

before them. Here were exquisitely carved chairs, regal beds and a glistening throne overlaid with gold. Over there were delicate alabaster vases and a brightly painted chest. Before them were three huge gilt couches, their sides carved into the shapes of strange animals. Lord Carnarvon ran his hand along the back of one, which seemed to be part crocodile and part lioness, with the head of a hippopotamus, its ferocious jaws open wide.

"The great goddess Ammut," Carter murmured, "who devours the souls of the wicked."

Lady Evelyn turned her light to the left and gasped. A pile of the broken bodies and wheels of several golden chariots seemed about to tumble on her. "It's as if there had been some horrible crash!"

"There was no accident," said Carter. "Tomb robbers must have thrown them aside in their search for gold."

To their right, still standing guard at one end of the room, were two life-sized statues of a king. They held their maces and staffs before them forbiddingly. The gold of their skirts, sandals and headdresses gleamed, and from each forehead a sacred gold cobra reared up as if to strike.

Their minds whirling, the four agreed to continue exploring the next day.

In the morning, Callender set up electric lights in the chamber. In their glare, wonder quickly gave way to curiosity. Carter peeked into one of the chests—it was filled with ancient linen clothing of the finest quality and elegant sandals.

"Look, a snake!" cried Lady

THE ANIMAL COUCHES OF THE TOMB

The first things Carter saw when he entered the tomb were three gilded couches in the shapes of animals *(top)*. One had lion's heads *(above left)*, another the heads of cows *(above right)* and a third was in the shape of the goddess Ammut *(right)*, part crocodile, part lioness, part hippopotamus. To this day Egyptologists cannot say for certain what the couches were used for.

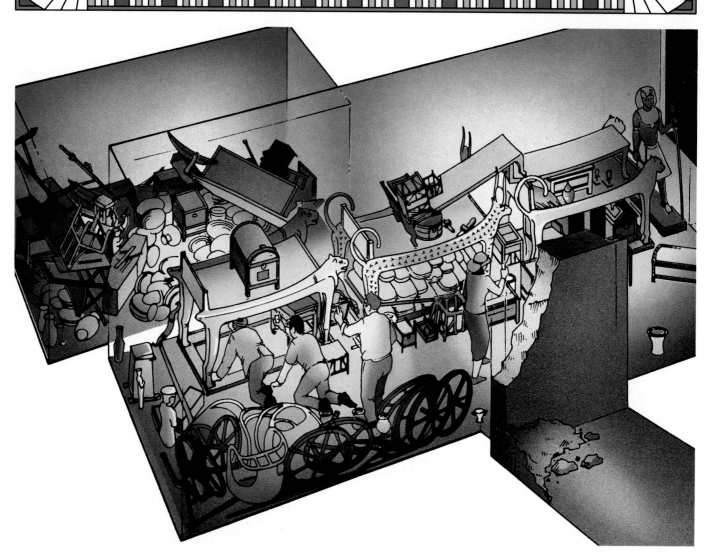

When Lord Carnarvon knelt under one of the animal couches *(above)* he spotted a hole in the wall leading to another chamber. This richly decorated chair *(right)* was one of the many objects found in the jumble of the next room.

Evelyn with delight at the sight of a carving of a great gilded reptile peeping out from a black shrine.

Carnarvon was down on his knees, peering under one of the great couches. "Here's a hole in the wall—it seems to lead to another room." Carter joined him and through the hole they saw a smaller room cluttered with pottery wine jars, alabaster vessels, baskets of fruit, stools, chairs and bedsteads.

Carnarvon looked at Carter. "Why would these rooms be in such confusion?"

"Thieves again," Carter replied. "But they didn't get away with everything. What I'm wondering is why we haven't glimpsed a coffin or a mummy."

"Maybe this isn't Tutankhamun's tomb after all. Maybe it's just a cache of objects hidden away by the ancient priests," Callender suggested.

While the three men gathered around the hole in the wall, Lady Evelyn explored the first chamber. "This looks

like the entrance to another room," she observed, running her fingers along the uneven surface of one wall. Between the two royal statues was another plastered area the size and shape of a doorway. Like the first two, a part of this doorway looked as though it had been opened and resealed. Carter's heart jumped.

"There must be more—what we've seen so far is just the beginning!" Carter needed time to think. He reeled at the prospect of the fabulous artifacts that might lie on the other side of the doorway, but it was too late to begin taking down the door that day.

They all climbed back into the passageway, and Carter and Callender reclosed the hole they had made. Carter instructed the watchmen on duty that night to guard the tomb with their lives, and then the four of them mounted their donkeys and rode out of the valley in a daze.

They talked about their discoveries late into the night. "We've got to find out what's inside that third room,"

Through the hole in the wall *(top)*, Lord Carnarvon saw a heap of jars, baskets, boxes and furniture *(above)*. Carter explained that ancient tomb robbers had emptied chests and boxes and tossed their contents around the chamber in a search for gold.

Carter said urgently. "Then we'll know whether or not we really have Tutankhamun's tomb."

After a moment's heavy silence, Carnarvon said, "I suppose there wouldn't be too much harm in a little investigation. But we'd have to keep it quiet—we don't want to give anything away to the newspapers yet. They won't pay to publish a story when everyone already knows how it ends!"

Carter nodded quickly, his eyes gleaming, and smiled at Callender. He was already planning their next visit to the tomb.

"I'm coming too," declared Lady Evelyn.

No one slept much that night. Their minds turned with all they had seen and all they might yet see in the sealed rooms. Long after the others had gone to bed, Carter sat up writing in his diary. For him, this had been "the day of days, the most wonderful that I have ever lived through, and certainly one whose like I can never hope to see again."

In this scene from the golden wall of one of the burial shrines, Tutankhamun *(center)* has arrived in the world of the gods and is presented by Maat, the goddess of truth *(right),* to Re-Harakhty *(left),* the sun god who carries the disc of the sun on his head.

The next night four donkeys wound their way back up the valley. Their riders were quiet, speaking only now and then in hushed, hurried whispers. Reis Ahmed Gurgar came forward to meet them as they neared the excavation site, shielding a lantern with his hand. "The guards have been dismissed," he told Carter. "I'll wait here for you." And then in a lower voice he added, "Be careful, Mr. Carter. This is a sacred place."

Moments later, Carter, Carnarvon, Lady Evelyn and Callender stole down the dark steps into the passageway. They entered the now familiar first room and Callender switched on the lights. "Eve, stand at the door and listen for anyone coming until we're through the wall," Carnarvon said.

Taking a chisel in his hand, Carter gently tapped at the resealed section at the bottom of the doorway. He felt the piercing gaze of the two royal statues as he worked. The plaster gave way quite easily, and soon he had made an opening large enough to squeeze through. Crouching down on all fours, Carter poked his head in and then inched his way forward. Carnarvon and Lady Evelyn followed.

"Hold on, wait a minute," the rather large Arthur Callender whispered hoarsely. "I don't think I can make it through such a small hole."

But the others didn't hear him. Once through the entrance, they faced what seemed to be a wall of gold! As Lord Carnarvon and Lady Evelyn shook the dust from their

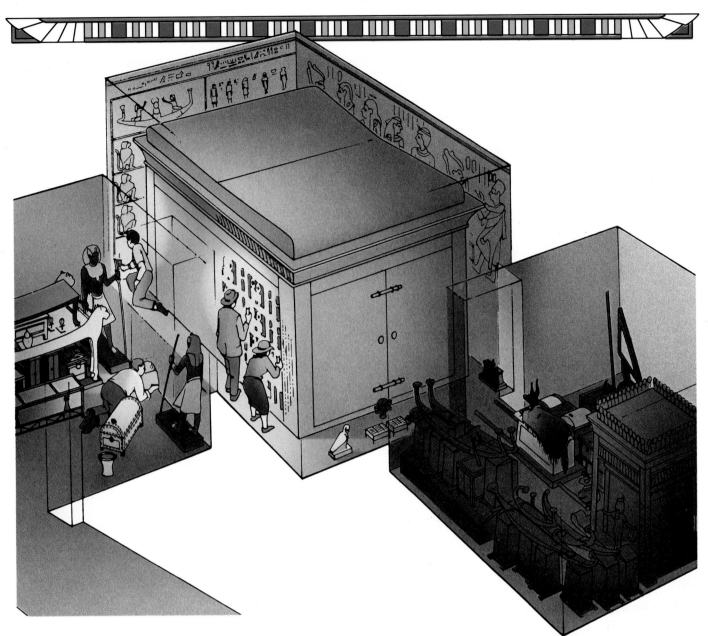

clothes, Carter made his way along this wall to the edge of the room. He realized that the small chamber was almost entirely filled by a large gilded shrine. "There's no doubt now. It's the burial chamber," he declared.

He noticed two ebony bolts holding the doors of the shrine shut and glancing at Carnarvon, who nodded back, Carter carefully pulled them. Nothing happened. He tried once again, then, slowly, the two huge doors swung open. Behind them was another gilded shrine draped with a brown linen shroud. The doors of the second shrine were tied shut just as the priests had left them thousands of years before.

"We've got Tutankhamun—intact." Carter's voice broke as he looked around at Carnarvon and Lady Evelyn.

Their secret visit to the tomb had told Carter what he so desperately wanted to know—that the mummy of Tutankhamun still lay undisturbed within the burial

Carter, Carnarvon, Lady Evelyn and Callender made a secret midnight visit to the burial chamber, but Callender didn't see beyond the burial shrine that night: he was too large to fit through the hole in the door.

chamber. One by one Carter, Carnarvon and Lady Evelyn squeezed back through the hole in the wall which Carter covered with a large basket lid. The official opening of the first chamber was due to take place the next morning. No one must know that they had already explored the tomb.

As the four explorers rode back down the valley, Carter pondered on all that he had seen. Ancient tomb robbers had clearly burrowed into the burial chamber, but they must not have had time to disturb the mummy. How would the mummy look after more than three thousand years? What riches would be buried with it? And why, he wondered, had the boy king been buried in such a small tomb?

CHAPTER THREE

TREASURES FROM THE TOMB
THE VALLEY OF THE KINGS 1922-1923

This alabaster jar with a crouching lion on its lid contained face cream used by the young pharaoh.

The next day Carter, Carnarvon and Lady Evelyn sat on the cool verandah of Carter's house trying to imagine how the ancient robberies had occurred.

It was clear that the outer doorway of the tomb had been opened and repaired twice—so there must have been two separate robberies. The fact that the repairs on the doorway had been stamped with the seals of the ancient priests seemed to indicate that all the plundering had been done within a short time of the king's burial.

"The robbers could have witnessed the funeral or even been among the burial party, who knows?" Carter said. "On the night of the robbery they probably met in the valley after dark. Then they would have had to drug or bribe the royal tomb guards. They must have worked very quickly, hammering at the blocked doorways, tearing the stone and plaster away with their hands until they had made an opening big enough to slip through. When those first robbers came, the passage leading to the tomb was empty, so it would have been easy for them to reach the first chamber."

"Of course. There were those bits of gold and the bronze arrowheads you found underneath the rocks in the corridor," said Lady Evelyn. "They must have been dropped by the first set of thieves on their way out and covered by rubble later."

"That's right," Carter continued. "The thieves probably searched in a frenzy for valuables that they could carry away with them—breaking pieces of gold off the furniture and the chariots which were too cumbersome to cart off. They seem to have taken linen and cosmetics as well."

"They left plenty of evidence. There's that cosmetic jar with fingerprints in the ointment—maybe one of them tested a little, just to see if it was worth taking," Carnarvon laughed. "And there's also that white wooden box with dirty footprints on it. No doubt they belonged to an ancient thief."

"Yes," Carter agreed. "Perhaps the first set of robbers didn't get beyond the first and second chambers. Just before sunrise, the lookout probably called to them, and they would have hurried out of the tomb, staggering under the weight of their plunder.

"My theory is that once they discovered that the tomb had been robbed, the royal officials were in a hurry to put

Howard Carter personally supervised the moving of each of the priceless artifacts from the tomb to the nearby laboratory.

things back into order," he continued. "They filled the corridor with rubble to protect the tomb from more robberies. The second group of thieves would have had to dig a tunnel through all those rocks."

"So they had to work for their booty—just like us," Lady Evelyn said, smiling at her father. "It must have taken them ages."

"Once inside they explored the entire tomb," Carter said, caught up in his version of what might have happened. "It's clear from the mess those jewel boxes were in that they made off with a lot of what was left of the valuables.

"But at least one of those thieves met with some bad luck. Remember, we found eight gold rings wrapped in a scarf in one of the boxes in the first chamber. I suspect someone was caught in the act and tried to get rid of the evidence quickly. After the second robbery, the tomb seems

to have been tidied up in a hurry before it was resealed."

"According to what I've been reading, if they were caught the robbers' fate would have been a grim one," Carnarvon said. "Apparently tomb robbers were impaled on a sharpened stake. They must have had nerves of steel to risk such a death."

"Let's just hope we don't have any unwelcome visitors," Carter frowned. "We have reliable guards, but I'll only rest easy when the steel bars are in place."

Once Carter knew that Tutankhamun's mummy lay undisturbed in the burial chamber, he wanted nothing more than to break the seal on the second shrine. He imagined over and over again the moment when he would lift the lid of the coffin and gaze upon the face of the pharaoh.

But he knew that before he could reach the mummy, a huge task lay ahead for the excavation team. Before exploring the other chambers of the tomb, Carter wanted

AN EGYPTIAN TREASURE.

THE WONDERFUL DISCOVERIES IN EGYPT

LORD CARNARVON'S OWN COMPLETE ACCOUNT.

NEW CAVE OF ALADDIN

MATCHLESS WORKS OF ART

We are able to print to-day a complete account the Earl of Carnarvon of the wonder ancient royal...

Sensational newspaper headlines (above) brought visitors from around the world hoping for a glimpse of the treasures as they were brought out of the tomb. Sometimes so many of them crowded around the work site that Carter was afraid they would all tumble into the tomb entrance.

to empty the first chamber, keeping precise records of everything he found. Clearing and studying one object at a time from the tomb was the best way to learn about the burial customs of the ancient Egyptians. He also hoped that by working in one chamber at a time, he could prevent precious objects from being accidently damaged by the many people who would have to pass through the first chamber on their way to the rest of the tomb.

Carter and Arthur Callender stood in the first chamber surveying the heaps of treasure around them.

"There's so much work to do. I don't know of an archaeologist in the world who has ever had such a mammoth task ahead of him."

Callender could see his friend was feeling the strain of the job and tried to calm him. "Well, what do we need first?"

"That's easy. What we really need is an instant excavation team—a conservation expert, specialists in reading hieroglyphs, draftsmen, a cataloguer, a photographer, guards...."

Luck was with Howard Carter. He received a telegram from the curator of the Egyptian Department at New York's Metropolitan Museum of Art. The cable congratulated him on his fabulous discovery and offered to help him in any way possible. Carter lost no time in answering: DISCOVERY COLOSSAL AND NEED EVERY ASSISTANCE. Within weeks Carter had a team of experts to help him. The tomb, which had lain in silence for thousands of years, became a noisy hub of activity.

The excavators' job was made especially difficult by the sweltering heat in the valley. Though it was winter in Egypt, temperatures would soar to 100°F (38°C). Carter, his temper already made short by the heat, found himself under pressure from journalists who clamored to get into the tomb. They were furious because Lord Carnarvon had signed a contract giving *The Times* of London the first opportunity to report on anything to do with the discovery. Even the Egyptian newspapers would have to wait to hear news of what was happening in their own country.

The site was plagued by tourists who arrived as early as the workers and gathered around the entrance to the tomb all day. They could be as pesky as flies with their questions and demands for a guided tour. Some of them even claimed to be Carter's long-lost relatives in the hope that he would let them in.

This colorful chest *(below)* found in the first chamber *(far left)*, was the first object to be removed from the tomb. Inside it Carter found a robe and sandals *(left)* that belonged to the king.

Finally the team was ready to remove the first big object from the room—a wooden chest exquisitely painted with hunting and battle scenes.

"All right, Harry, I'm ready for you," Carter called out.

Harry Burton, the team's photographer, entered the chamber and took pictures of the chest where it sat. Meanwhile, the draftsman drew a picture of it on his floor plan of the first chamber. Callender and Carter then gingerly lifted the chest onto a padded wooden stretcher and secured it with bandages. They carried it up the corridor and stairs where they were met by a guard.

As Carter and Callender emerged from the darkness of the tomb with their precious load, the sunlight shone brightly on the painted chest. There were loud whistles and squeals of delight from a crowd of tourists who had arrived hoping to catch a glimpse of the ancient treasures.

"Would you look at that paint job!" a man with a large camera said.

"Beautiful!" someone else exclaimed. "I wonder what's inside?"

But Carter and Callender had no time to stop and answer questions as they pushed their way through the crowd. They would have to repeat this time-consuming procedure for the hundreds of other objects in the first chamber before they could open the sacred shrines. And once spring came, it would be too hot to even set foot in the valley.

They carried the chest over to their lab which had been set up in an empty tomb nearby. There Carter and his assistant spent days carefully emptying the chest, which held a pair of rush sandals in perfect condition, a gilded headrest and royal robes of a size that would fit a young boy.

Soon after it was removed from the tomb, the wood of the chest began to shrink and parts of the precious painted surface started to peel off. Carter knew that this was because the cool, dry air in the lab was a shock after three thousand years in the warm, humid tomb. To prevent further damage, the chest was coated with wax. After it had been treated, it was photographed once again then packed for the journey to Cairo.

The clearing did not always go as smoothly as Carter had hoped. A pair of beaded sandals on the floor of the chamber looked like they were in perfect condition. But when Carter tried to pick one of them up, it crumbled to dust, leaving him holding a handful of beads. Horrified, Carter decided that some of the objects would have to be conserved on the spot. He poured melted wax on the other sandal, and once it had hardened he was able to pick it up quite easily.

Inevitably, there were some disappointments. What Carter had thought was a box of papyri—ancient records written on reed paper which might clear up the mysteries of Tutankhamun's reign—turned out to be full of nothing but underwear for the young king.

In January when Lord Carnarvon and Lady Evelyn returned to the valley, Carter took them directly to the lab. The smell of chemicals nearly knocked them over. Carnarvon was in high spirits, and while Lady Evelyn poured glasses of champagne for the hot, tired excavators, he looked over the treasures which had been recently cleaned and conserved. He clapped Carter on the back. "These things look even more beautiful than they did when we first set eyes on them. You've done a fabulous job, Carter!"

Carter smiled wanly, and politely waved away the glass that Lady Evelyn held out to him. "No, thank you. Too much to do."

A few weeks later everything had been cleared out of the first room except for the regal statues standing guard at the entrance to the burial chamber. Another official opening, this time of the burial chamber, was about to take place. All of Luxor seemed to know about it—the name of Tutankhamun was on everyone's lips. Twenty guests had been invited including Egyptian royalty and foreign ambassadors, and chairs had been set up for them in the now nearly-empty first room.

"I must admit Carter, I'm a little nervous that someone's going to find out we've already been in there," Carnarvon confessed in hushed tones outside the tomb. It was just after two o'clock and the guests, lavishly dressed as if going to a party, had already gathered inside and were waiting for Lord Carnarvon and Howard Carter to give their speeches. A large crowd of uninvited guests and journalists had gathered around the stone wall outside the tomb.

"So am I. But Callender and I have built up that small platform hiding the place where we entered. And I'll start chipping away at the door from the top. Once we're inside everyone will be too excited to notice," Carter

OPENING THE BURIAL CHAMBER

Carter and Carnarvon had to pretend that they were as curious as their guests on the day of the official opening of the burial chamber.

1) Carter placed reeds and a basket lid over the hole he had made in the wall of the burial chamber on the night of their secret entry.

2) Carter (right) and Carnarvon (left) stand on the platform they built to conceal the secret entry hole.

responded, straightening his shirt.

"I hope you're right," muttered Carnarvon, going down the stairs to the tomb. "If the newspapers find out we already know what's in there, it will take all the suspense away."

As the guests watched, Carter put on a pair of heavy gloves, picked up a crowbar and began to chip away at the plaster doorway leading to the burial chamber. Piece by piece he, Lord Carnarvon and their assistants removed the stones. The excitement and suspense in the room were almost unbearable.

Ten minutes later Carter had made a large hole. He peered in with a flashlight and saw once again the magnificent wall of gold. Then he set about widening the hole so that they could enter the chamber. The stones were heavy and it was a good two hours before the blocking could be removed.

The head of one of the statues that stood guard outside the burial chamber.

At last Carter and Carnarvon stepped down through the opening. Their eyes met briefly as they remembered their first secret entry into the chamber a few months before.

When they reached the great doors of the shrine Carter drew back the ebony bolts revealing the doors to the second shrine with its seals intact. They bore the name of Tutankhamun. He touched the seals longingly—if only he could break them open now.

But then Carter felt a slight chill. They were intruders in the presence of the dead king. No one uttered a word for a minute or two. A large bouquet of flowers reminded them that the last people to stand inside this tomb had probably been the young king's friends and family, bidding him a last farewell.

Carnarvon said, "Come, Carter, we ought to let our guests have a look." (*continued on page 39*)

3) It took hours before the heavy stone blocks in the doorway could be removed. Then Carter *(left)* and Carnarvon *(right)* climbed through the hole and into the burial chamber for the second time.

4) The world's first look at the dazzling blue and gold shrine which contained three more golden shrines and a stone sarcophagus holding the coffins and the mummy of the king.

"WONDERFUL THINGS!"

"Never before in the whole history of excavation had such an amazing sight been seen," wrote Howard Carter of his first glimpse into the tomb. The treasures he found in Tutankhamun's tomb remain without equal to this day.

Carter found this alabaster chalice *(right)* inside the door of the Antechamber where it had been dropped by escaping thieves. He called it the "wishing cup" because the inscription on it contains a wish for Tutankhamun's eternal happiness.

1

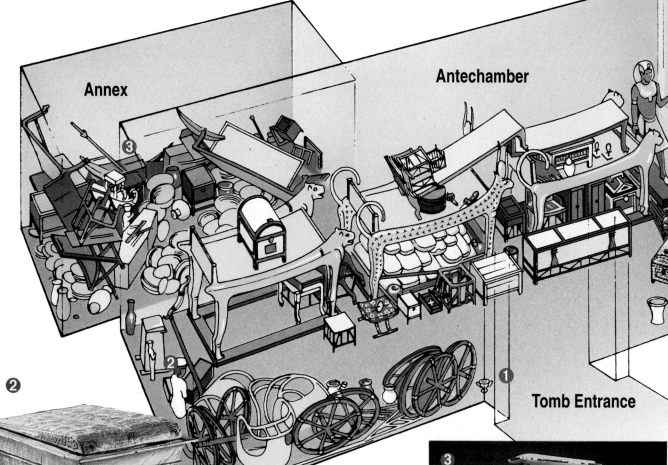

Annex

Antechamber

3

2

2

1

Tomb Entrance

3

This dazzling golden shrine *(left)* once contained a statue of the king, but this too had been stolen by the tomb robbers. *(Right)* An elaborate boat carved from alabaster was probably a table centerpiece. At the front and back of the boat are ibex heads with real ibex horns.

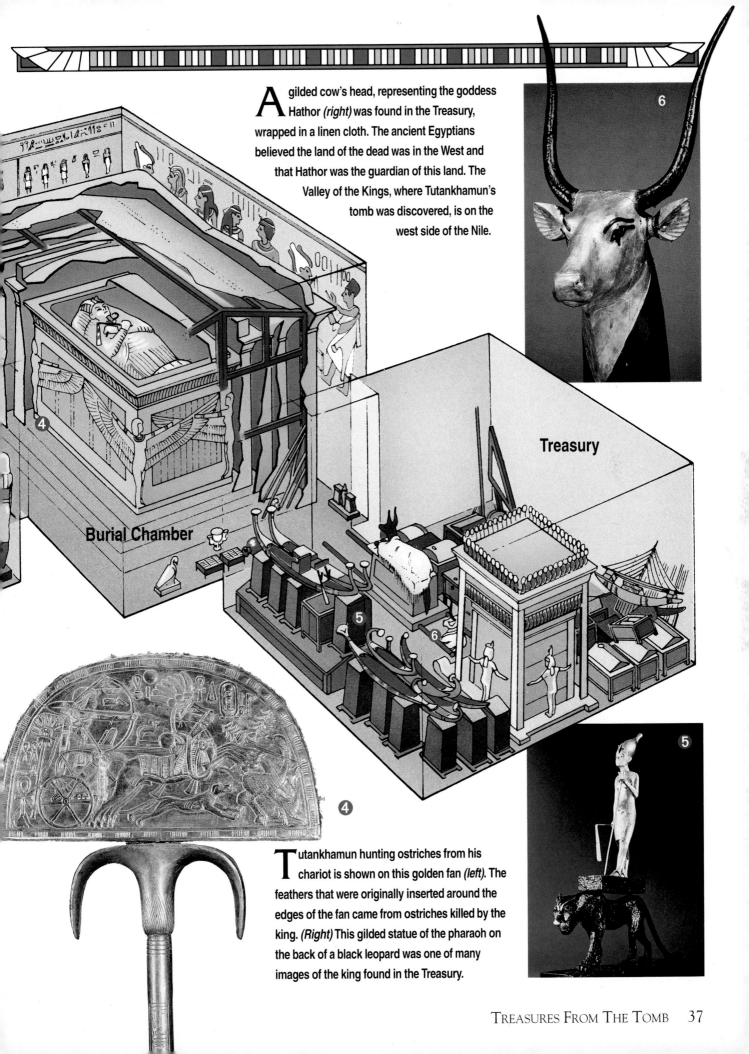

A gilded cow's head, representing the goddess Hathor *(right)* was found in the Treasury, wrapped in a linen cloth. The ancient Egyptians believed the land of the dead was in the West and that Hathor was the guardian of this land. The Valley of the Kings, where Tutankhamun's tomb was discovered, is on the west side of the Nile.

6

Treasury

Burial Chamber

4

5

6

5

4

Tutankhamun hunting ostriches from his chariot is shown on this golden fan *(left)*. The feathers that were originally inserted around the edges of the fan came from ostriches killed by the king. *(Right)* This gilded statue of the pharaoh on the back of a black leopard was one of many images of the king found in the Treasury.

THE RICHES OF THE TREASURY

The ancient Egyptians believed that in order for a person's spirit to survive in the next life, every part of the body had to be preserved by mummification. Internal organs, which would quickly decay if left in the body, were taken out, dried, wrapped in linen, placed in jars, then put in a sacred shrine *(below)*.

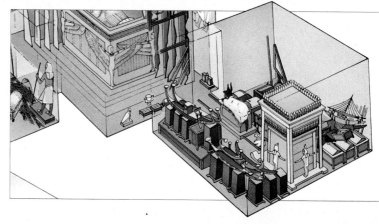

The graceful figure of the goddess Selket *(right)* was one of four goddesses keeping eternal watch over the shrine containing the internal organs of the king.

This elegant statue of Anubis, the jackal god of embalming *(right)*, with its gilt ears and eyes and silver toenails, guarded the entrance to the Treasury *(top)*. According to ancient Egyptian myths, Anubis made the first mummy and by doing this showed how eternal life could be possible for everyone.

Inside the sacred shrine was this chest carved out of alabaster *(above)*. Within were four compartments, each with a lid shaped like a pharaoh's head *(below)*.

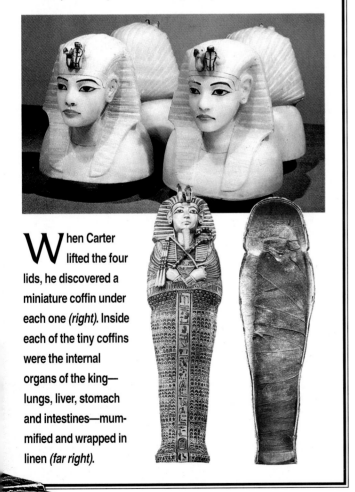

When Carter lifted the four lids, he discovered a miniature coffin under each one *(right)*. Inside each of the tiny coffins were the internal organs of the king—lungs, liver, stomach and intestines—mummified and wrapped in linen *(far right)*.

The Treasury held many miniature model boats which were meant for Tutankhamun's use in the next life.

(*continued from page 35*)

"Wait! Here's another chamber!" Carter exclaimed. The men made their way a little further along the wall until they reached a low doorway and then edged their way past the elegant black Anubis dog guarding the entrance to the room. They had seen this fourth room on their secret visit to the burial chamber, but in the excitement of discovering the unopened shrines, hadn't taken the time to explore it.

Carter caught his breath when he saw a gilded shrine-shaped chest, delicately modelled with the figures of four guardian goddesses. It was the most beautiful monument he had ever seen in all his years as an archaeologist and it brought a lump to his throat.

"This probably contains the king's embalmed internal organs—the liver, lungs, stomach and intestines," he said.

Carter lifted the lid of a wood casket. Inside was an ostrich feather fan with an ivory handle. "This is in perfect condition—it's as though the tomb were only closed yesterday," he marveled. The room was full of fascinating objects including a number of black shrines and chests. They were all sealed except for one in which Carter could see statues of Tutankhamun standing on the backs of black leopards. And scattered everywhere were model boats for the king to use in the afterlife. There were canoes for hunting hippos and birds as well as ceremonial vessels for making holy pilgrimages. Some of the boats had linen sails and rope rigging.

The men emerged from the burial chamber, their eyes

unbearable heat of the Egyptian summer forced them to close it down.

One scorching day Carter left the site earlier than usual, returning to his house for lunch. Shortly afterwards Lord Carnarvon arrived, eager to discuss his last meeting with the Egyptian authorities. "They are being impossible," he complained to Carter. "After all the money I've poured into this excavation they have the gall to tell me that all of the objects should stay here in Egypt."

"Well, perhaps they should, my lord, as national treasures."

"Come, Carter, not you too. I know you feel the same way about this as I do. I'm not insisting that I should take *all* the artifacts back to England with me, but a man should have something to show for his work."

"All I know is that if I were an Egyptian, I would hate to see any of the treasures leave my country," Carter continued stubbornly. "It would be a crime if the contents of the tomb were to be divided."

"But you know perfectly well that the whole lot would still be buried in the desert if it hadn't been for me," Carnarvon replied.

Carter, who had been pacing the room, turned on Carnarvon. "I do hope that my own small efforts haven't gotten in your way!"

Lord Carnarvon gripped his cane. He had seen Carter in a rage before,

Tutankhamun accepts flowers from his young wife, Queen Ankhesenamun *(above)*. Perhaps it was the grieving queen who placed this bouquet *(right)* in the tomb where it was found by Carter and Carnarvon over three thousand years later.

shining. Two by two the guests were invited to climb through the opening and look at the wonders within.

As the excavation season drew to a close, the days became hotter and hotter and there were frequent dust storms in the valley. Carter was tense and exhausted, but still he pressed his team on. He wanted to clear as much of the tomb as possible before the

but it had never been directed at him. "What? Everyone knows how much credit you deserve. I think this heat is getting to us all, my good man," he said, trying to remain calm. "I know you don't mean what you're saying about giving the Egyptians everything. Perhaps we'd better discuss this another time."

Carter glared at Carnarvon, his face red with fury. "I meant exactly what I said," he shouted. "And I mean this

THE MUMMY'S CURSE

Lord Carnarvon *(below)* died just four months after the discovery of Tutankhamun's tomb. Some people believed the real cause of his death was not pneumonia, as was listed on his death certificate *(bottom right)*, but the mummy's curse. The hand of the mummy, they believed *(top right)*, would reach out from the tomb to strike down anyone who dared to disturb it. Some

eerie coincidences gave support to this belief. When Lord Carnarvon died, the lights went out all over Cairo and his favorite dog back in England howled and dropped dead. Strangest of all, when Tutankhamun's mummy was unwrapped in 1925, it had a wound on its left cheek in exactly the same place

where Carnarvon received the insect bite that became infected and led to his death.

But if there really was a "mummy's curse," why were the people closest to the work on Tutankhamun's tomb never affected? Lady Evelyn lived until 1980. Howard Carter, who the mummy might have been most eager to kill, lived for seventeen years after the tomb's discovery and died of natural causes in 1939.

too—get out of my house, and don't bother coming back again!" Carter stormed out of the room, slamming the door behind him.

A month later Carter received a letter from Lady Evelyn. Lord Carnarvon was seriously ill. He had been bitten by a mosquito, Lady Evelyn wrote, and had nicked the bite with his razor while shaving. Blood poisoning and fever had set in. After a few days her father had seemed to get better, but had then suffered a relapse and come down with pneumonia. Her mother, brother and the family doctor were on their way to Egypt.

Lord Carnarvon died a few days later on April 5, 1923. He did not live long enough to see the mummy of the pharaoh he had waited so many years to find.

Carter sat on the shaded verandah of his house thinking about Lord Carnarvon. He missed his friend a great deal, and bitterly regretted their final argument.

"Tea, Mr. Carter?" Abdul Ali asked, walking out onto the verandah with a laden tray in his hands.

"Thank you, Abdul."

"At the site they say Lord Carnarvon was struck by the mummy's curse," Abdul said as he poured. "He has been punished because he opened a sacred royal tomb."

"That's superstitious rubbish. There isn't any curse on the tomb."

"I'm not so sure," the servant replied. "They say the lights went out all over Cairo the night Lord Carnarvon died. And you yourself told me that his favorite dog howled and dropped dead in England at the same time."

"Those are coincidences, Abdul. Nothing but coincidences."

"And the cobra killing your canary, Mr. Carter? Was that a coincidence too?"

Carter stared off into the distance toward the Valley of the Kings. Abdul wasn't the only one who seemed convinced that they might all be touched by the mummy's curse. He shook off the thought. "Nonsense," he muttered to himself as he watched the last rays of the sun climb the pink cliffs, leaving the valley in deepest darkness.

CHAPTER FOUR

INSIDE THE BURIAL CHAMBER
THE VALLEY OF THE KINGS, EGYPT, 1923-1924

Carter was greatly relieved when, after her husband's death, Lady Carnarvon decided to renew the license to dig in the Valley of the Kings under her own name. He knew that years of work still lay ahead of him and it would have been unbearable for him if he had not been the person to open the pharaoh's shrines.

The second season began in October 1923. The first thing Carter did was remove the two life-sized guardian statues of the king which remained in the first chamber. Then he and Arthur Callender began to take down the wall dividing the first chamber from the burial chamber.

The doors of the third shrine were still tied shut and stamped with the unbroken seal of the ancient priests when Carter found them.

The ancient Egyptians had constructed this wall to separate the two rooms once they had maneuvered the huge shrines into the burial chamber.

"How I miss Carnarvon," Carter said to Callender as they chipped away at the wall. "I never realized how much time he spent dealing with the newspapers and the authorities. He knew how to keep them happy. Now it's all up to me, and I'm not having much luck."

"They hardly leave us time to get any work done," sympathized Callender. "What's the latest?"

"The same old things, really," Carter replied. "Newspapers all over the world are upset because we're letting *The Times* have first news of what we're finding. The Egyptian authorities are edgy because they're under pressure from their own newspapers, who don't like to see their national treasures in the hands of Englishmen.

"Then there are all those visitors they want me to let in. We hardly have room to move in here! And there's still the question of who all these treasures will belong to. According to our license, Lord Carnarvon was to be given half of them. But it looks like most will stay here in Egypt. I just wish I could be allowed to concentrate on my work."

Once they had removed the wall, Carter could admire the full beauty of the enormous gilded shrine. Its dazzling

Howard Carter and members of his team peer into the shrines of the pharaoh *(above)*. On the wall of the third shrine was the image *(left)* of one of the gods the ancient Egyptians believed lived in the next world.

(Top) Inside the four golden shrines was a huge golden-yellow stone sarcophagus holding the coffins. Each of the four corners of the sarcophagus was decorated with an elegant winged goddess.

(Above) Carter wondered why there was a crack in the sarcophagus lid and why it hadn't been properly repaired.

blue and gold walls were decorated with the sign that meant "life." Before he could examine the inner shrines, he and his team had to take apart and remove the heavy pieces of the first shrine. Since the outer shrine fitted closely around the one inside it, the team had to work layer by layer. This was no easy task in the cramped, stuffy burial chamber. The men constantly bumped their heads and pinched their fingers as they worked.

Weeks later came the moment that every archaeologist dreams of. A small group of the excavators gathered in the burial chamber as Carter rolled back the fragile shroud covering the second shrine. He drew back the bolts at the top and bottom of the second shrine and held the sealed cord tightly. He carefully cut the cord and slowly opened the doors.

Inside was yet another shrine—the seals on its doors were also intact.

"That makes three. How many more can there be?" asked Callender.

"There's much more to come," whispered Carter. He knew from an ancient papyrus document describing another royal burial that there could be as many as five shrines nestled inside one another.

The doors on the third shrine were also sealed. Carter drew the bolts, neatly cut the cord and opened the doors to find a fourth shrine, covered with hieroglyphs. There were no seals holding these bolts fast. His heart beating faster and faster, Carter drew back the ancient bolts and the doors slowly swung open.

The small crowd of onlookers standing behind Carter gasped. Filling the fourth shrine was a huge golden-yellow stone sarcophagus, its lid firmly in place, just as it had been left when the tomb was sealed. For a few moments they all stood silent in respect.

But Carter couldn't stand still for long. His eyes drank in the sarcophagus which was decorated with the exquisitely carved figures of four winged goddesses. He ran his hand along the lip of the lid. "It's just as the ancient priests left it." But then his brow clouded.

"What is it?" asked Callender.

"There's a crack here, right across the top. It has been patched, but I wonder why they didn't replace it. In fact, this lid is made of a different stone from the sarcophagus. So much in this tomb seems to have been done in a hurry."

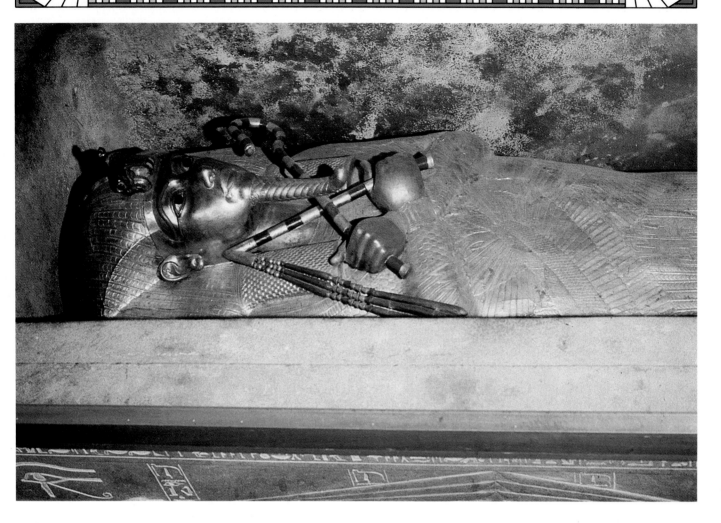

When Howard Carter lifted the cracked stone lid of the sarcophagus, he saw the first of three magnificent golden coffins.

"Solid stone," remarked Callender. "It must have taken a dozen men to lift it. How on earth are we going to open it in this tiny space?"

"With difficulty," Carter replied with a sigh. "We'll have to remove all of the shrines before we can take off the lid and look inside."

Taking out the three remaining shrines was almost as difficult as moving the first one had been. As his excavation team dismantled the heavy, fragile panels, Carter was puzzled by what he saw. The guide marks on the doors of the shrine showed that they were meant to face west. Instead they faced east and the side panels had been put on the wrong way. Someone had ruthlessly banged together some sections with a hammer, making deep dents in the beautiful gilt work. Wood chips had been carelessly left behind by the ancient workmen. Why had the sacred shrine been treated so badly?

Carter looked nervously around the table at the many archaeologists and government officials. It was February 12, 1924, the day of the official opening of the sarcophagus, and lunch had been prepared by the Winter Palace Hotel and brought to the Valley of the Kings.

After lunch the group crowded into the burial chamber and gathered around the sarcophagus. Carter glanced anxiously at the complicated tackle which they had set up to raise the sarcophagus lid. It seemed to be in working order. The crowd was silent. Harry Burton's movie camera began to whir as the workmen put their shoulders to the ropes.

Carter held his breath as the heavy stone lid trembled and then rose, swinging clear of the sarcophagus. He gripped its edge and peered inside, his eyes slowly adjusting to the darkness within the great box. At first all he could see were a few pieces of stone that had chipped off the lid, but then a dark shroud became visible.

Slowly, carefully, Carter rolled back two pieces of ancient linen. Everyone crowded around in wonder.

Before them lay the shining golden image of the boy king

The ancient Egyptians filled their tombs with food and drink so that the spirits of the dead could feast in the next world.

on a magnificent coffin in the shape of a mummified body. On the pharaoh's head was the royal headdress, with the cobra and vulture, showing that he was king of Upper and Lower Egypt. His arms were crossed, and he carried the two symbols of Egyptian royal power—the crook and the flail.

The coffin was huge. "There must be more coffins inside it," Carter said to those around him.

Soon Callender began to direct the crowd out to an empty tomb nearby where tea had been set up to celebrate. As they walked to the tomb Carter noticed one of the government officials. Hurrying to catch up with him, Carter said, "I'd like to show the wives of the excavation team what we've seen today. Would it be all right if they had a brief look before we let the press in tomorrow?"

The Egyptian authorities were becoming stickier every day. They had respected Lord Carnarvon's wishes, but Carter found himself clashing with them at every turn. He didn't have Carnarvon's gift for keeping the peace.

"I don't see why not," responded the official stiffly. "But I'll just check with the Minister to make sure."

Tired by the endless, polite chatter, Carter was only too glad when the guests and officials began to leave. He found himself drawn, irresistibly, back to the burial chamber. There the face on the coffin gazed back at him. It was proud but peaceful. He noticed a tiny wreath of flowers around the cobra and vulture on the pharaoh's forehead and wondered if it might have been left there by Tutankhamun's young queen. At that moment she seemed very near. He could almost feel her presence in the burial chamber beside him.

The next morning about an hour before Carter was scheduled to take the wives of the team members into the burial chamber, a donkey rode up to the house, stirring up clouds of dust. It was a messenger from the Egyptian government.

"I'm terribly sorry, sir," he said, handing Carter an official envelope. "But I have orders here that you are to let no one

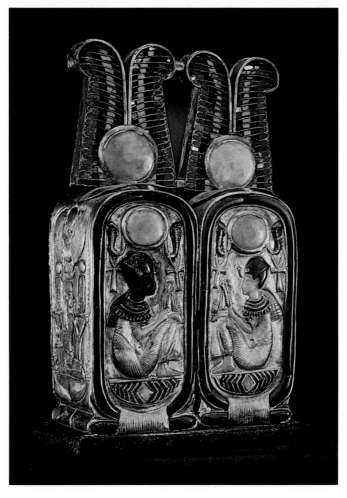

TOMB LOCKED AGAINST MR. CARTER.

LUXOR SURPRISE.

GOVERNMENT GUARD POSTED.

A deadlock has been reached in the Valley of the Kings at Luxor, where on Tuesday Mr. Howard Carter opened the sarcopha... the Pharaoh Tut...

(Left) This gorgeous ointment container shows the king as he was in life *(right)*, and as he would be when reborn *(left)*. The reborn king was shown as black on the left because black was the color that symbolized new growth and new life to the ancient Egyptians. *(Above)* The news that Carter had been locked out of the tomb made headlines in newspapers around the world.

into the tomb today except for members of the press."

"What...," Carter spluttered tearing open the envelope.

He was furious. He'd had enough of the whims of the authorities. Here was proof that all they wanted to do was to insult him and the excavation team. How dare they, he thought to himself in a rage, after all the work we've done on the tomb. He showed the letter to his friends. Together they agreed that they should walk off the job.

Taking the only set of keys, Carter rushed to the site. He slammed shut and padlocked the steel gates to the tomb and the lab. Inside the burial chamber the heavy lid of the sarcophagus still hung in the air above the precious gold-covered coffin.

"Reis Ahmed!" shouted Carter. His head foreman appeared and Carter explained what had happened. "I want you to stay here and guard the tomb. I'll be back as soon as I can."

"But the lid of the sarcophagus..." the foreman began. Carter didn't even seem to hear him as he jumped into his car. He went straight to the Winter Palace Hotel in Luxor and posted a notice:

OWING TO THE IMPOSSIBLE RESTRICTIONS AND DISCOURTESIES OF THE EGYPTIAN PUBLIC WORKS DEPARTMENT AND ITS ANTIQUITY SERVICE, ALL MY COLLABORATORS, AS A PROTEST, HAVE REFUSED TO WORK ANY FURTHER UPON THEIR SCIENTIFIC INVESTIGATIONS IN THE TOMB.

Because of Carter's hasty actions the Egyptian authorities cancelled Carter's and Lady Carnarvon's right to excavate in the valley. Forcing Reis Ahmed Gurgar to step aside, government guards broke in and took possession of the tomb. Inside the burial chamber the ropes holding the heavy lid of the sarcophagus had stretched so far that it almost brushed the coffin. The authorities carefully lowered the lid and announced that they would continue work at the site. And, to Carter's horror, they began to let hundreds of people visit the tomb every day, without providing proper security for the priceless treasures inside.

Carter left Egypt a short time later, convinced that he would never see the royal tomb again.

CHAPTER FIVE

THE MUMMY IS REVEALED
THE VALLEY OF THE KINGS, EGYPT, 1925

"**M**r. Carter!" Reis Ahmed cried, rushing down the crowded platform of the Luxor train station.

Carter struggled to get off the train with his heavy load of luggage. He could hardly believe his eyes when he saw his loyal foreman. He had been away from Egypt for nearly a year now, yet Reis Ahmed had managed to find out when he was returning and had come to meet his train just as he always used to do.

"It's good to be back," Carter said, shaking Reis Ahmed's hand vigorously. "How's everything at the tomb?"

"Ready for us to begin work again," the foreman responded proudly.

While Carter was out of Egypt, the government had changed. A new minister was now in charge of archaeological digs, and he had renewed Lady Carnarvon's license to continue work at the tomb of Tutankhamun. Everyone had recognized that there was no archaeologist better able to do the job than Howard Carter, and there was great relief all around when he returned to Egypt.

But the clearing of the tomb would now take place under a different set of conditions. Lady Carnarvon had

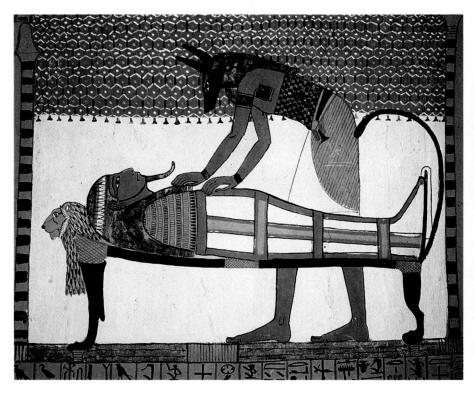

The jackal-headed Anubis, god of embalming, places a portrait mask on a mummy he has finished wrapping.

agreed to let all the ancient treasures remain in Egypt. And the contract which gave *The Times* first news of any discovery was cancelled.

Despite Reis Ahmed's assurances that none of the precious objects in the tomb or in the lab had been damaged, Carter's stomach churned as they drove up into the valley. His time away from Egypt had been filled with nightmares about thousands of people going through the

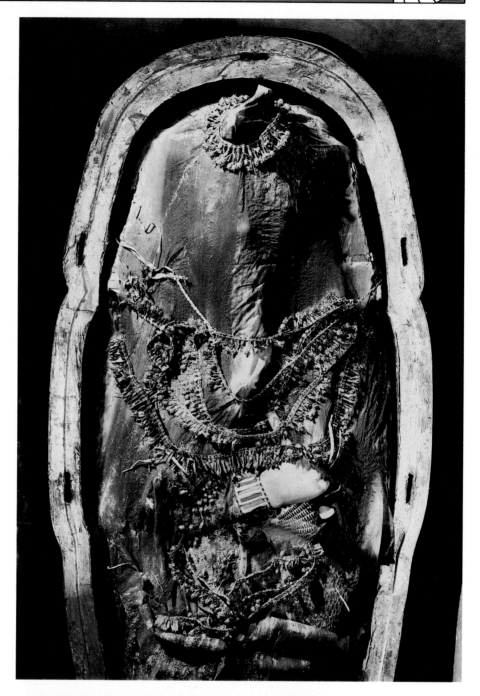

chambers, handling the artifacts, dropping and breaking the fragile alabaster, slipping smaller pieces of jewelry into pockets. Was it possible that he would find everything as he had left it?

The valley looked more beautiful than ever. The sun was sinking quickly and the hills and cliffs cast long shadows. Soon tiny stars appeared, growing brighter as the sky became a deep purple.

In near darkness Carter quickly inspected the tomb and lab. He breathed a sigh of relief when he saw that almost nothing had been touched. Outside the lab he found the ancient linen pall which had covered the second shrine. It had been left outside, and as he and Ahmed picked it up, it fell to pieces. "This is a great shame," Carter said sadly, holding the crumbling cloth in his hands, "but at least nothing else seems to have suffered."

Several months later, the moment Carter had waited so long for arrived. He was ready to open the gilded coffin.

Carter, Arthur Callender and the other members of the excavation team gathered around the open sarcophagus. After attaching pulley blocks to the four silver handles on either side of the coffin lid, they slowly raised it. Inside, garlands of cornflowers, blue lotus petals, and olive and willow leaves had been strewn over a linen shroud.

Carter carefully removed these. Underneath was another coffin showing the image of a king in shining gold. It was even more magnificent than the first!

"So much care and respect for the

(Above) When Howard Carter lifted the lid from the first coffin, he found the second coffin wrapped in a linen shroud. The second coffin had to be pulled out of the first with ropes and pulleys before its lid could be removed (left).

THE COFFINS OF THE BOY KING

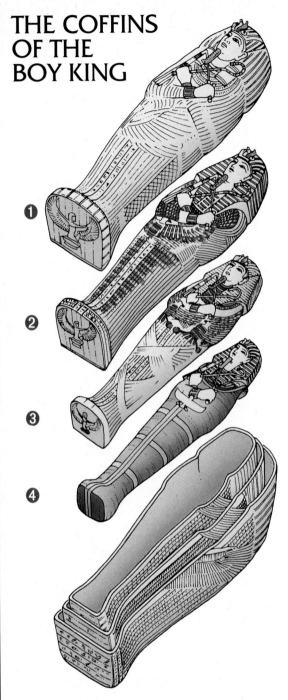

① **1)** Tutankhamun's first coffin was made of wood covered with a thin layer of shining beaten gold. *(See page 45.)*

② **2)** The second wooden coffin was also covered with beaten gold and inlaid with brilliantly colored glass. *(See above right.)*

③ **3)** The third coffin was made of solid gold. *(See page 53.)*

④ **4)** The king's wrapped mummy was decorated with gold bands, a gold mask and hands of sheet gold. *(See pages 54 and 55.)*

dead pharaoh," marveled Callender. "And see how tightly the coffins fit, nestled inside one another like Russian dolls."

"They didn't leave us much elbow room, did they?" said Carter. "We'll have to lift the coffins out of the sarcophagus before we go any further, I think."

Using pulleys, they hoisted the first coffin and its contents free of the sarcophagus. It took eight men pulling on the ropes with all their strength to lift it.

"What on earth could make this so heavy?" said Callender in amazement, mopping his brow with his handkerchief.

Carter bent over the second gold-covered coffin and gently brushed away bits of linen from the face. Around the pharaoh's neck was a falcon collar of red, blue and turquoise glass. The entire golden surface of the mummy-shaped coffin was decorated with an elaborate feather pattern inlaid with bright glass, but Carter noticed that some of the pieces of inlay were loose.

"That's probably due to dampness," said Callender.

"Let's just hope it hasn't damaged the mummy, too," Carter replied.

When the men removed the lid of the second coffin they saw the red linen shroud that had been carefully tucked around a third coffin. Only the burnished gold face of this coffin had been left uncovered. On top of the shroud was a collar made of glass beads, leaves, flowers, berries and fruit. With trembling hands Carter removed the fragile collar and lifted the red linen. His heart almost stopped.

The richly decorated second coffin was big enough to hold a third coffin, inside which lay the mummy of the king.

The third coffin was made of solid gold!

The men were speechless for a few moments, as they took in the sight before them. "Can you imagine how wealthy the ancient pharaohs must have been? No wonder the tombs were irresistible to thieves," Carter exclaimed. He had never even dreamed of finding anything so splendid.

"And no wonder it was so heavy," Callender added.

The third coffin was the most richly decorated of the three, with necklaces and a falcon collar inlaid with semi-precious stones. Exquisite winged goddesses decorated its body. Their outstretched arms encircled the body of the king protectively. Much of the decoration was hidden by a black pitch-like substance which had been poured over most of the coffin.

"Whatever is that?" asked Harry

The face on the second coffin lid *(above)* was so different from the faces on the other two that Howard Carter believed it had been made for someone else. The lid of the second coffin *(left)* opened to reveal a third coffin wrapped in a red linen shroud.

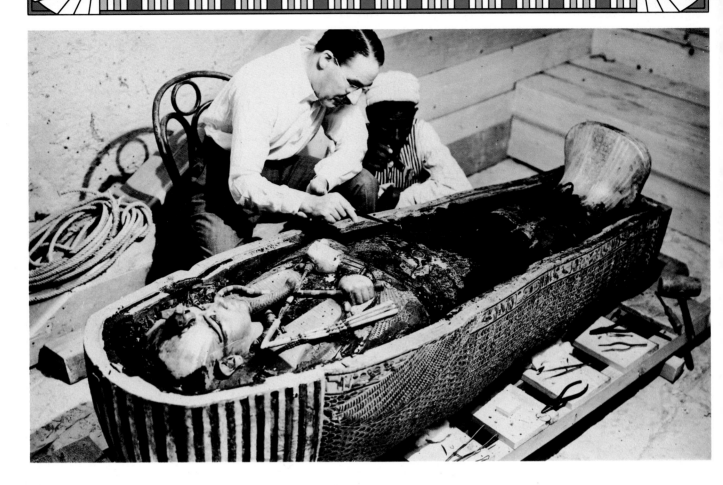

Before he could open the third coffin, Carter had to carefully chip away a layer of black pitch which had been poured on the coffin and left to harden for centuries.

Burton as he moved about the chamber, setting up for the next photograph.

"It must have been some sacred oil," guessed Carter. "But it has dried as thick as tar. Unfortunately so much of it was used that this coffin seems to be stuck inside the bottom of the second one."

A hush fell over the group in the burial chamber as Callender and Carter and two other members of the team grasped the handles on the lid of the solid gold coffin, lifted it and set it to one side.

There, inside the shell, lay the body of the king.

Carter could see that it was neatly wrapped in linen bandages. These were held in place by decorated gold bands. The mummy was covered with the same oils that they had found on the outside of the coffin.

Tutankhamun's mummy bore a magnificent mask of burnished gold, which covered its face and shoulders. Its headcloth was inlaid with blue glass. The vulture and cobra

on its forehead, ready to spit fire at the pharaoh's enemies, were of solid gold. The face on Tutankhamun's mask looked sad and gentle. It was, Carter thought, the face of one who had not expected death to come so soon.

Sheet gold hands holding the crook and the flail had been sewn onto the mummy's bandages. Across the mummy's chest lay a large golden bird, its wings spread wide as if in flight. It was a sacred image of the king's spirit. The Egyptians believed that at death the spirit flew free, but that it returned to the body when it was ready to enjoy eternal life. That was why they took care to fill tombs with everything necessary for a rich and happy afterlife. And that was why mummifying their dead was so important to them. The body had to be perfectly preserved so that the spirit would recognize it when it returned to the tomb.

Because the same black pitch that had covered the gold coffin had been poured over the mummy, the body as well as the mask were stuck to the inside of the casket. The men carried the heavy coffin outside, hoping that the hot sun would melt the hardened pitch, but it didn't. They would have to examine the mummy in its coffin.

The medical examination of the mummy took place on

November 11, 1925. Carter had called in two anatomy experts, Dr. Derry and Dr. Hamdi, to perform the operation.

"I'm afraid it's not in very good condition," Dr. Derry warned Carter after a brief look at the bandaged form. "The skin underneath may be brittle."

Sure enough, the bandages crumbled at a touch. The two doctors decided to strengthen these wrappings with wax before making the first incision.

Carter had an uneasy feeling as the scalpel was poised above the mummy. Should we be doing this, he asked himself. From the first moment that he, Lord Carnarvon, Lady Evelyn and Arthur Callender had entered the royal tomb he had been struck by the great care and compassion with which the ancient Egyptians had laid their young pharaoh to rest. What right had he to undo their loving work?

But at the same time Carter understood that clearing the tomb and unwrapping the mummy were vital because of what they would reveal about Egyptian life. His work over the past few years had shown the world how this ancient civilization buried their royal dead. He was adding rich knowledge to the pages of history books.

He knew, too, that once news of the treasures and the mummy reached the world they would never have been left untouched inside the tomb. Had they fallen into the hands of modern tomb robbers, they would have been lost forever or damaged beyond repair.

Dr. Derry made a shallow cut into

(Above) The third coffin was made of solid gold and inlaid with precious stones. The foot of the coffin was carved with this image of the goddess Isis with her wings outstretched **(left)**.

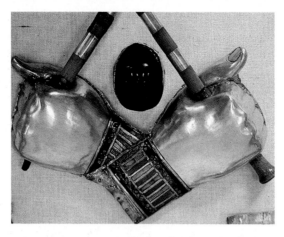

Tutankhamun's linen-wrapped mummy was decorated with gold ornaments. Hands of sheet gold *(right)* were sewn on to its chest and its head was covered with this gold mask, the most magnificent ever found *(below)*. Carter believed that the mask showed an exact likeness of the king's face.

the layers of bandages from the bottom of the gold mask down to the feet and folded the decayed wrappings back. It was impossible to remove a single piece of bandage intact.

"We won't be able to tell exactly how the mummy was bound," Carter frowned.

"No," agreed Dr. Derry. "But you can see that the fingers, toes, arms and legs were all individually wrapped before being enclosed in the bandages that went around the whole body."

Carter bent down with a magnifying glass to look at the inner wrappings. To his disappointment they were like soot. Even so, he could see that the very finest linen had been used closest to the king's body.

As the men removed the brittle bandages from the body of the mummy they found more than a hundred jewels and amulets—charms whose magical powers would protect the young king from the dangers of the underworld. Around his neck were layers of collars and pendants. His folded arms were encircled by bracelets inlaid with semi-precious stones. On his fingers were thirteen rings. His feet were encased in gold sandals and a set of gold sheaths protected his toes. At Tutankhamun's waist was a gold-handled dagger with a blade made of iron, a metal rare in his day and prized for its strength.

When all the bandages were removed Carter could see that Tutankhamun's body was cracked and brittle. The skin was a grayish color and the limbs shrunken and thin. Carter noticed the place where the ancient embalmers had made their incision on the left side of the stomach to remove all of the

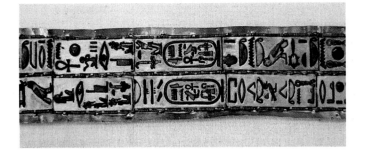

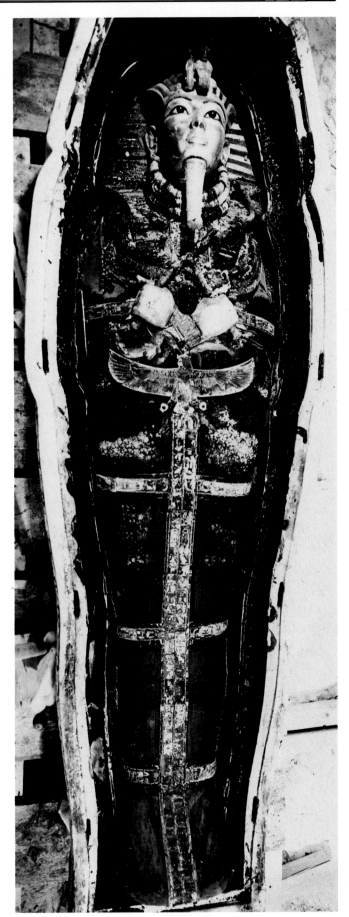

(Right) Inside the third coffin was the mummy of the king. The gold bands which surrounded the linen wrappings *(above)* are inscribed with a wish for the pharaoh's safe passage into the next world.

king's precious internal organs.

Before the mummy's head could be examined the doctors had to remove the gold mask. Because the head was still stuck fast to the gold mask, the doctors finally had to separate the two by sliding heated knives between them. After removing a few layers of wrappings they could see that the king wore a delicate gold headband. More bandages were slowly removed—they had to be very careful with the fragile mummy.

At last Carter found himself face to face with the boy pharaoh.

In the dry and fragile skin he could read the features he had seen in the handsome gold mask. Tutankhamun wore an elaborate beaded skull cap on his shaven head. The king's eyes were open, and Carter could see that he had had long eyelashes. His nose had been flattened by the pressure of the bandages. Strong, white teeth showed through his parted lips.

After studying Tutankhamun's fragile bones, Dr. Derry and Dr. Hamdi were able to say that the young king had been 5' 5 1/8" (1.65 m) tall. He had had a slight build and was about eighteen years old when he died.

"How do you think he died?" Carter asked.

"I'm not sure," Derry replied. "It does seem strange that he was so young. There's no evidence that I can see of disease. I suppose he might have had an accident…or maybe even have been murdered."

"We do know when he died though," said Callender. "The flowers we found in the tomb only bloom in March or April, so it must have happened early in the year."

Long after the others had gone, Carter stood in the tomb looking down at Tutankhamun's mummy. He turned Dr. Derry's words over in his mind. Accident? Or murder?

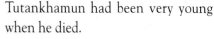

It was fashionable for wealthy boys to wear earrings in ancient Egypt and Tutankhamun was buried with several pairs *(above)*. Holes are still visible in the mummy's ears *(right)*.

Before they were wrapped in linen, each of Tutankhamun's toes was encased in a sheath of gold *(right)* and sandals made of beaten gold were placed on his feet *(above)*.

Tutankhamun had been very young when he died.

Carter thought of all the unusual things he had noticed since the clearing had begun—the fact that the tomb was so small, the simple wall paintings in the burial chamber which hardly seemed fit for a king, the fact that the shrine had been hastily put together the wrong way around and the pieces carelessly banged into place. The face on the second coffin, it now struck him, was not the same as the faces on the other two. Had it been intended for someone else and adapted for the boy king at the last moment?

Was it possible that Tutankhamun had been murdered? Could one of his power-hungry guardians have cut short the reign of the boy king? And if so, had the tomb and burial goods been thrown together in a hurry before anyone could investigate?

As he wearily climbed the steps out of the tomb into the cool night air Carter thought of Lord Carnarvon. How sad it was that he had not been there to share the greatest moment of this discovery.

But Carter also felt that Tutankhamun had somehow escaped him. The centuries had taken their toll on the body of the king. He thought of the golden spirit bird which had been laid over the mummy. Where was Tutankhamun's spirit now, he wondered. Had it recognized the king's body when it returned to the tomb? Was Tutankhamun now pharaoh once more, surrounded by all his treasures in the afterlife? Or was his spirit without a home, soaring high in the night sky above the Valley of the Kings?

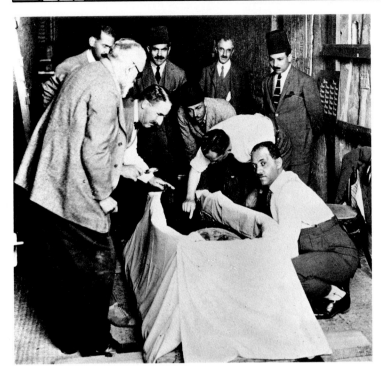

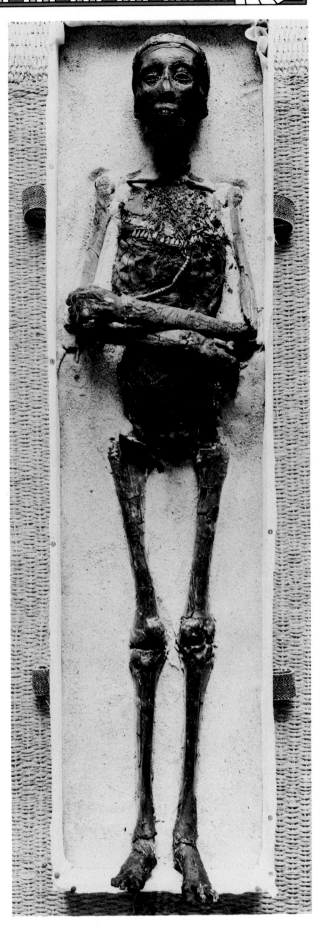

Howard Carter and the medical team *(above)* unwrapped and examined the body of King Tutankhamun *(right)*.

This vulture-shaped collar *(above)* was draped around the mummy's throat and the daggers *(left)* were found near its waist.

THE TOMB'S SECRETS
HAMPSHIRE, ENGLAND, 1988

I spent much of my first day at Highclere Castle fitting together the fragile wood fragments we had discovered. By evening the two ancient jewel boxes looked much as they had thousands of years ago. I still had months of work ahead of me, but my task was small compared to what Howard Carter had been faced with.

After examining the mummy, Carter worked at Tutankhamun's tomb for more than seven years. First he cleared the Treasury, which was full of religious objects. He then moved on to the small room where the tomb robbers had made such a mess. There he found a wealth of supplies including food—bread, lentils, berries, raisins, honey, spices and almonds—meant to keep the young pharaoh well nourished in the afterlife.

It was not until ten years after the first stone step was uncovered that Carter finished the enormous task of clearing the thousands of treasures from the tomb and packing them up for the journey to the museum in Cairo. When he finally returned to London he began to write a long, detailed account of his work on Tutankhamun's burial place. He wanted to tell other archaeologists about what he had found and the techniques he had used in the excavation of the tomb.

(Above) One of the wooden jewel boxes found in pieces at Highclere Castle *(top)*. *(Right)* The magnificent gold death mask placed on Tutankhamun's mummy.

Unfortunately, Carter became ill and never finished his book. Though his name had once appeared in every newspaper, he was almost forgotten in his last years and he died a lonely man in 1939. Only a handful of people attended his funeral—one of them was Lady Evelyn.

I drove away from Highclere Castle just as dusk was beginning to fall, still thinking about the discovery of Tutankhamun's tomb. Lord Carnarvon's wealth and his interest in Egyptology combined with Howard Carter's expert knowledge and his determination had brought to light the greatest archaeological treasure in history. The tomb of Tutankhamun was the first royal burial place ever to be discovered intact. No pharaoh before or since has been found in such splendor, within his stone sarcophagus and his gilded coffins, in the very tomb where he had been laid after his death.

And never before had a tomb been cleared so carefully. Carter gave loving attention to each object no matter how small or insignificant it might have seemed. He knew that every item had a story to tell. He made detailed notes and accurate drawings of everything he found. Thanks to the methodical way Lord Carnarvon and Howard Carter cleared Tutankhamun's tomb, the discovery has given us

THE GUARDIANS' SECRET

The two life-sized statues of Tutankhamun found in the Antechamber *(below)* were meant to provide bodies for his spirit to inhabit in case anything were to happen to his mummy. But they may have had yet another purpose. Ancient records written on papyrus, like the fragment from another tomb found at Highclere Castle *(top inset)*, may be hidden in the skirts of these statues *(bottom inset)*. If they are found, perhaps they will tell us more about ancient Egyptian religion and burial customs.

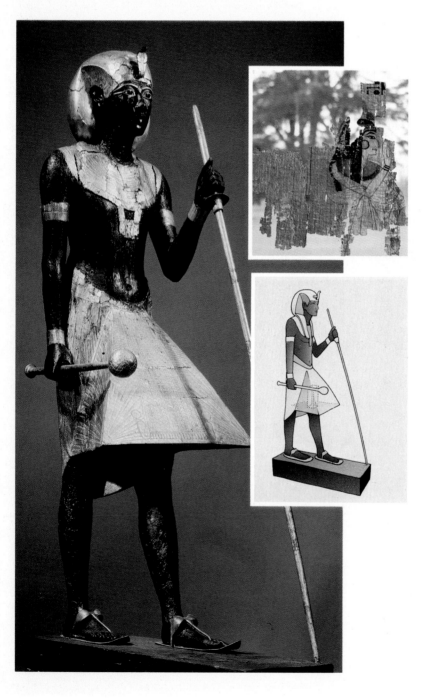

invaluable knowledge about the burial practices of the ancient Egyptians, and shown us their fine craftsmanship. Because time and money were lavished on the precious objects, people will be able to enjoy them for centuries.

But Howard Carter was never completely satisfied with his discovery. He had hoped that the mummy would be in better condition so that he would be able to determine the cause of the young king's death. In 1968, x-rays of the mummy's skull revealed a loose fragment of bone, suggesting, perhaps, that Tutankhamun received a blow on his head. But whether this occurred before or after his death and whether it was accidental or intentional remains a mystery.

Carter was also disappointed that he found no papyrus rolls in the tomb to tell him more about Tutankhamun's reign. I believe, however, that we may find them soon. In the British Museum there is a guardian statue from another Egyptian tomb that seems once to have had a papyrus roll hidden inside it. It struck me one day that Tutankhamun's guardian statues might also contain such ancient records. Their construction is identical to the one in the British Museum, and it even looks to me as though the skirts of Tutankhamun's guardian statues have a secret opening underneath. Perhaps the missing religious texts of Tutankhamun will be recovered when my colleagues and I begin work on the statues. Maybe they will explain why Tutankhamun went back to worshipping the old gods.

The most exciting thing about the discovery of Tutankhamun's tomb and

Pharaoh Tutankhamun and his queen enjoy a quiet afternoon in their splendid garden pavilion in this scene from the back of the pharaoh's golden throne.

the more recent finds at Highclere Castle is how they link our lives with those of the ancient Egyptians. The wooden jewelry box I had admired today had been held by someone who lived thousands of years ago. The riches buried with Tutankhamun bring us face to face with the boy king. His burnished gold mask shows us what he looked like. From the metalwork on his beautiful golden throne and the scenes painted on boxes we can see that he enjoyed the company of his young wife and that he loved to hunt. The personal objects that Carter found in the tomb—the games, the food, the sandals, even a lock of Tutankhamun's grandmother's hair—open a window on the young king's

daily life. All of a sudden he is more than just a name in our history books. He has become flesh and blood.

The treasures from Tutankhamun's tomb toured the world for many years. But the constant packing and unpacking began to wear on the precious objects and so they were returned to the Egyptian Museum in Cairo. The mummy of Tutankhamun still lies inside the outermost coffin in his tomb in the Valley of the Kings where it has rested for more than three thousand years. There it is visited by millions of people.

The ancient Egyptians believed that if their names were remembered and repeated after their deaths, they would live on in the afterlife. Because of Lord Carnarvon and Howard Carter's magnificent discovery, Tutankhamun's story is known throughout the modern world. Every time we speak his name, his wish for eternal life comes true.

GLOSSARY

alabaster: A white stone through which some light can pass.

antiquity: An object produced in ancient times.

archaeology: The scientific study of people from the past and their cultures. An *archaeologist* is a person who studies archaeology.

artifacts: Objects made by the people of an ancient culture.

British Museum: A museum in London, England, famous for its large collection of Egyptian artifacts.

burnished: Made shiny from polishing.

Carnarvon: Lord Carnarvon was the title given to Henry Herbert by King George III of England in 1780. Since that time, the title has always been passed to the eldest son of the family upon the death of his father. The Lord Carnarvon who discovered Tutankhamun's tomb was the fifth Lord. His grandson, the present Lord Carnarvon, is the seventh.

conserve: To clean and repair ancient objects to prevent them from being damaged in the future.

draftsman: A person skilled in drawing plans and sketches.

dig: A term referring to a search conducted by archaeologists for ancient buildings or artifacts they believe are buried under the ground.

ebony: The hard, black wood from a tropical tree.

Egyptologist: An archaeologist who studies ancient Egypt.

embalm: To treat a dead body so that it will not decay. *Embalmers* were the people who preserved the dead bodies.

excavate: To dig for ancient buildings, tombs or artifacts.

foreman: The chief workman in a group. The foreman supervises the work of the others.

gilded: To be covered with a thin layer of gold.

hieroglyphs: The picture writing of the ancient Egyptians.

ibex: A wild mountain goat with large, curving horns.

ivory: The hard, creamy-white material that forms an elephant's tusks.

jackal: A type of wild dog.

mace: A heavy stick carried by a king or high official.

mummy: The body of a person or animal that has been preserved by drying.

natron: A coarse, grainy salt found in deposits beside the Nile River and used in the embalming process to remove moisture from bodies.

papyrus: A tall plant that grows in Egypt. The paper made when the stem of this plant is cut into strips and pressed together is also called papyrus.

pharaoh: A ruler of ancient Egypt. The word pharaoh comes from a word meaning "the great house," which described the palace where the pharaoh lived.

rubble: Loose fragments of stone.

rush: A tall, thin plant that grows beside the water.

sarcophagus: A huge stone box containing a coffin or coffins.

shrine: A large decorated box that holds a holy object or the remains of an important person.

shroud: The cloth used to cover a dead body or a shrine.

Sotheby's: A company which holds auctions where art and ancient artifacts are sold.

tackle: A series of ropes and pulleys used to lift a heavy object.

temple: The place where gods are worshipped.

Tutankhamun: The ruler of Egypt from 1332 B.C. to 1323 B.C. Tutankhamun was only about nine years old when he became ruler and he died mysteriously at the age of approximately eighteen.

HOW MUMMIES WERE MADE

The ancient Egyptians believed that after death their spirits would travel to another world during the day, and at night would return to their bodies. In order for a person's spirit to live forever, it had to be able to recognize and return to the body. If a spirit couldn't recognize the body it belonged to, it would die. That is why the Egyptians wanted to preserve the bodies of their dead in as lifelike a state as possible. Mummification guaranteed eternal life for the spirit.

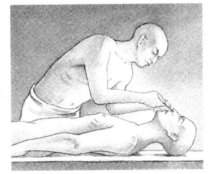

1 After the body had been washed with wine and spices, all of the parts that might decay were removed. The embalmers first removed the brain through the nose using a long hook. Next they made a deep cut in the abdomen and took out the internal organs: the lungs, the stomach, the liver and the intestines.

2 The body was stuffed with bundles of a strong drying salt called natron. It was then completely covered with natron and placed on a slanted embalming couch so that any fluids that dripped out as the body was drying could be collected and buried along with it.

3 While the body was drying, the internal organs were also dried and preserved with natron. They were then wrapped in strips of linen, placed in tiny coffins and put in a chest divided into four compartments. Each compartment had a lid with the face of a pharaoh.

4 After forty days the body, now completely dry and shrunken, was removed from the natron. The bundles of natron were taken from inside the body cavity and the whole body was washed inside and out with oil and fragrant spices.

5 The mummy's head and body were packed with linen soaked in scented oil so that they would regain the shape they had in life. Once this was done, the mummy could be covered with necklaces, rings and bracelets made of gold and gems.

6 The entire body was then covered in shrouds and bound with strips of linen until the mummy had returned to its original size. This was a complicated job and could take as long as a week. Small magical objects were placed between the layers of wrapping to protect the mummy's spirit on its way to the afterworld.

7 After the wrapping was finished, the head of the mummy was covered with a portrait mask, just to make sure that the spirit would recognize it. The masked mummy was then placed in a series of gilded wooden coffins and put into a sarcophagus.

RECOMMENDED FURTHER READING

The Complete Tutankhamun
by Nicholas Reeves — 1990
(Thames and Hudson Inc., U.S./Thames and Hudson Ltd., U.K.)
Egyptologist Nicholas Reeves tells the story of the discovery of the famous tomb and examines all the artifacts in detail.

Ancient Egypt
Eyewitness Books — 1990
(Random House, U.S./Dorling Kindersely Limited, U.K./Stoddart Publishing Co. Limited, Canada)
Every aspect of life in ancient Egypt, from the court of the pharaoh to the activities of ordinary people, is described and illustrated with full-color photographs.

In Search of Tutankhamun
by Piero Ventura and Gian Paolo Ceserani — 1985
(Silver Burdett Company, U.S./Macdonald & Co., U.K.)
This illustrated story of the discovery of Tutankhamun's tomb also provides useful information on ancient Egyptian religious beliefs and everyday life.

Ancient Egypt
by Daniel Cohen — 1990
(Doubleday, U.S., U.K., Canada)
Gary Lippincott's gorgeous paintings are the highlight of this account of life in ancient Egypt which includes the Egyptian system of writing, mummification, tomb robbers and a look inside Tutankhamun's tomb.

Mummies, Tombs and Treasure
by Lila Perl — 1987
(Clarion Books, U.S.)
Explains how and why the ancient Egyptians mummified their dead, details their beliefs about the afterlife and describes how almost every Egyptian tomb was robbed and the mummies destroyed.

PICTURE CREDITS

Front Cover: *(Top)* The Robert Harding Picture Library *(Bottom left)* Lehnert and Landrock *(Bottom middle, right)* The Robert Harding Picture Library
Front Flap: *(All)* The Robert Harding Picture Library
Back Cover: *(Left)* Painting by Stephen Hutchings *(Right)* Diagram by Jack McMaster/Margo Stahl *(Center)* © Kodansha Ltd.
Back Flap: Claire Reeves
Endpapers: The Robert Harding Picture Library
Page 1: Lee Boltin
3: © Kodansha Ltd.
4-5: The Robert Harding Picture Library
6-7: Painting by Stephen Hutchings
8-9: The Griffith Institute
10: *(All)* David Cunningham
11: *(Top)* Courtesy Highclere Castle *(Bottom)* Claire Reeves
12: *(Top)* The Times, Stephen Markeson *(Bottom)* Arnaud Carpentier
13: *(Top)* Courtesy Highclere Castle *(Left inset)* The Illustrated London News Picture Library *(Right inset)* Bettmann *(Bottom)* The Times, Stephen Markeson
14: Peter Christopher
15: *(Left, right)* Nicholas Reeves *(Inset)* Peter Hayman

16: *(Top)* Map by Jack McMaster/Margo Stahl *(Bottom)* C M Dixon
17: *(Left)* Diagram by Jack McMaster/Margo Stahl *(Right)* Peter Christopher
18: *(Top)* The Ancient Art & Architecture Collection *(Bottom left)* Nicholas Reeves *(Bottom right)* The Griffith Institute
20: The Times
21: *(All)* The Griffith Institute
22: *(Top)* The Griffith Institute *(Inset)* The Illustrated London News Picture Library
23: *(Left)* The Griffith Institute *(Right)* The Robert Harding Picture Library
24: Diagram by Jack McMaster/Margo Stahl
25: *(Top)* The Griffith Institute *(Middle left, right)* The Robert Harding Picture Library *(Bottom)* The Robert Harding Picture Library
26: *(Top)* Diagram by Jack McMaster/Margo Stahl *(Bottom)* The Ancient Art & Architecture Collection
27: *(All)* The Griffith Institute
28: The Robert Harding Picture Library
29: Diagram by Jack McMaster/Margo Stahl
30: The Robert Harding Picture Library
31: The Griffith Institute
32: *(Left)* The Times *(Right)* The Griffith Institute

33: *(Left, inset)* The Griffith Institute *(Right)* The Robert Harding Picture Library
34: *(All)* The Griffith Institute
35: *(Top)* The Robert Harding Picture Library *(Bottom left, right)* The Griffith Institute
36: Diagram by Jack McMaster/Margo Stahl *(Top, bottom left)* Lee Boltin *(Bottom right)* The Robert Harding Picture Library
37: *(Top)* The Robert Harding Picture Library *(Bottom left)* Art Resource *(Bottom right)* Bettmann
38: *(Top right)* Diagram by Jack McMaster/Margo Stahl *(Middle left)* Griffith Institute *(Middle right, bottom)* The Robert Harding Picture Library
39: *(Top left, bottom right)* The Griffith Institute *(Middle left, top right)* The Robert Harding Picture Library *(Bottom left)* Lee Boltin
40: *(Top)* The Robert Harding Picture Library *(Bottom)* UPI/Bettmann
41: *(Left, top right)* The Griffith Institute *(Bottom right)* Peter Hayman
42: The Griffith Institute
43: *(Top)* The Griffith Institute *(Inset)* Nicholas Reeves
44: *(Top)* The Robert Harding Picture Library *(Bottom)* The Griffith Institute
45: The Ancient Art & Architecture Collection
46: C M Dixon

47: *(Left)* Lee Boltin *(Right)* Nicholas Reeves
48: The Ancient Art & Architecture Collection
49: *(All)* The Griffith Institute
50: *(Left)* Diagrams by Jack McMaster/Margo Stahl *(Top)* The Robert Harding Picture Library
51: *(Top)* The Robert Harding Picture Library *(Bottom)* The Griffith Institute
52: The Griffith Institute
53: *(Top)* The Robert Harding Picture Library *(Bottom)* Nicholas Reeves
54: *(Top)* Nicholas Reeves *(Bottom)* The Robert Harding Picture Library
55: *(Top)* Nicholas Reeves *(Right)* The Griffith Institute
56: *(Top left)* Lee Boltin *(Top right, bottom right)* The Griffith Institute *(Bottom left)* The Robert Harding Picture Library
57: *(Top left)* The Mansell Collection *(Right)* The Griffith Institute *(Middle left)* Lee Boltin *(Bottom left)* The Robert Harding Picture Library
58: *(Top)* AA Photo Library *(Inset)* The Times, Stephen Markeson
59: © Kodansha Ltd.
60: *(Left)* The Robert Harding Picture Library *(Top right)* Arnaud Carpentier *(Bottom right)* Diagram by Jack McMaster/ Margo Stahl
61: The Robert Harding Picture Library
63: Diagrams by Jack McMaster